P9-DCL-921

★ ★ ★

THOMAS JEFFERSON

MILTON MELTZER

THOMAS JEFFERSON

The Revolutionary Aristocrat

Franklin Watts
New York/London/Toronto/Sydney

Frontispiece: Jefferson at fifty-six, drawn from life in Philadelphia, when he was vice president. The pencil sketch was made by Benjamin H. Latrobe.

Library of Congress Cataloging-in-Publication Data

Meltzer, Milton, 1915–
Thomas Jefferson: the revolutionary aristocrat / Milton Meltzer.
p. cm.
Includes bibliographical references and index.
Summary: A biography of the third president who was also the author of the Declaration of Independence.
ISBN 0-531-11069-9 (lib. bdg).—ISBN 0-531-15227-8
1. Jefferson, Thomas, 1743–1826—Juvenile literature.
2. Presidents—United States—Biography—Juvenile literature.
[1. Jefferson, Thomas, 1743–1826. 2. Presidents.] I. Title.
E332.79.M45 1991
973.4'6'092—dc20
[B] 91-15943 CIP AC

Printed in the United States of America
6 5 4

CONTENTS

ALSO BY MILTON MELTZER

Columbus and the
World Around Him

George Washington and the
Birth of Our Nation

Benjamin Franklin:
The New American

Mark Twain:
A Writer's Life

The Bill of Rights:
How We Got It and What It Means

The American Revolutionaries:
A History in Their Own Words

Voices from the Civil War

African-American History:
Four Centuries of Black Life
(with Langston Hughes)

American Politics:
How It Really Works

The Black Americans:
A History in Their Own Words

Starting from Home:
A Writer's Beginnings

All Times, All Peoples:
A World History of Slavery

Poverty in America

Crime in America

THOMAS JEFFERSON

★ ★ ★

INTRODUCTION

When we think of Thomas Jefferson, we see him as the lanky, freckle-faced young redhead sitting alone at a desk on the second floor of a boarding house in Philadelphia, penning the Declaration of Independence. That is the grand achievement which stands out in his legend, and one of the three he had chiseled on his tomb. (The others were his drafting of the Virginia Statute of Religious Freedom and the founding of the University of Virginia.) Note that he did not mention that he was third president of the United States. Anyone less modest would have been proud to list the many other things Jefferson could have rightfully claimed: his achievement as scientist, diplomat, agriculturist, architect, philosopher, educator.

What we know Jefferson best for are the eloquent words, his great pleas for freedom of speech and of the press, for democracy, for majority rule, for the right of revolution, for the abolition of slavery, for—in his everlasting phrase—"the right to life, liberty and the pursuit of happiness."

But like any one of us, Jefferson was a living, growing, changing person. He was always Jefferson, but not always consistent. Sometimes his actions contradicted his words. It might be because he came to change his mind. Or perhaps he was of two minds about a given issue, wavering now this way, now that. Or perhaps because there was a clash between what he felt was the ideal way to act and the pressures of the world outside. Both the worst of our presidents and the best (and Jefferson ranks high among the best) have sometimes become so heady with the power high office places in their hands that they violated the Constitution they have sworn to uphold.

This book cannot take up in detail every aspect of Jefferson's thought and work. It develops at greater length what concerns me most today. (Every biographer brings his own interests and biases to the subject.) Many scholars have explored in depth single facets of Jefferson's long life (he lived to be eighty-four). I have tried to provide the reader with some of the fruits of their research and their insights, as well as my own.

★ 1 ★

THE SHY SCHOLAR

In his earliest memory, little Thomas Jefferson is being carried on a pillow by a slave mounted on horseback. They were riding from the small wooden house where the boy was born to an elegant home 50 miles away where he would live for the next several years. That first recollection is a sort of symbol: Jefferson was supported by slave labor all his life, although he protested publicly that slavery was an evil America must get rid of. He owned several hundred slaves during his lifetime (and theirs); he liberated only a few, and he bought eight more slaves while he sat in the White House.

It was Virginia that Jefferson grew up in and always thought of as his "country." By the time of his birth (April 13, 1743) it was the largest American colony in size. It stretched as far west as the Mississippi and as far north as the Great Lakes. And largest in population. But the total colonial population was only 1.5 million. One-fifth of these people, or about 300,000 were black.

Early in the 1600s English settlers had found that Virginia's fertile soil and long growing season were well suited to tobacco. Its prodigious profits made tobacco the crop around which everyone's life revolved. In the competitive scuffle for success the winners acquired thousands of acres apiece.

But they could not work the vast tracts without exploiting the labor of others. At first they tried to get the Native Americans, whom they thought inferior to the whites, to till the fields. But when the Indians resisted, the planters began to force their removal. Now they turned to indentured servants, mostly young single men, brought over from England to work the tobacco farms for limited periods. It was a ruthless, militarized enterprise that created working conditions so terrible that nearly two-thirds of the laborers died before their terms were up. Gradually, after 1660, the planters shifted from the indentured system to a labor force of slaves from Africa.

Black men and women were uprooted from their African homeland, stripped of all rights, and treated as property. They came in chains, the cargo of an English monopoly called the Royal African Company. With the same contempt earlier generations of planters had shown for the American Indians and the English indentured servants, the masters created a slave code that gave them unlimited power over a labor force that could never be free.

When the colony's success seemed assured, the younger sons of the English gentry began to migrate to America. By the late 1600s they dominated Virginia's ruling elite. They held most of the county offices and controlled the legislature, called the House of Burgesses. Soon blood or marriage linked 90 percent of the burgesses. An aristocracy was born that would endure long after the American Revolution.

It was this class Jefferson sprang from. His father, Peter Jefferson, was a physical giant, in his mid-thirties when his son was born. Thomas's mother, Jane Randolph Jefferson, was twenty-three. Peter's own father had been a Virginia farmer, hunter, and surveyor. He died leaving some land and several slaves. He was not an educated man; few in the colony were at that time.

A label promoting one of Virginia's principal cash crops—tobacco

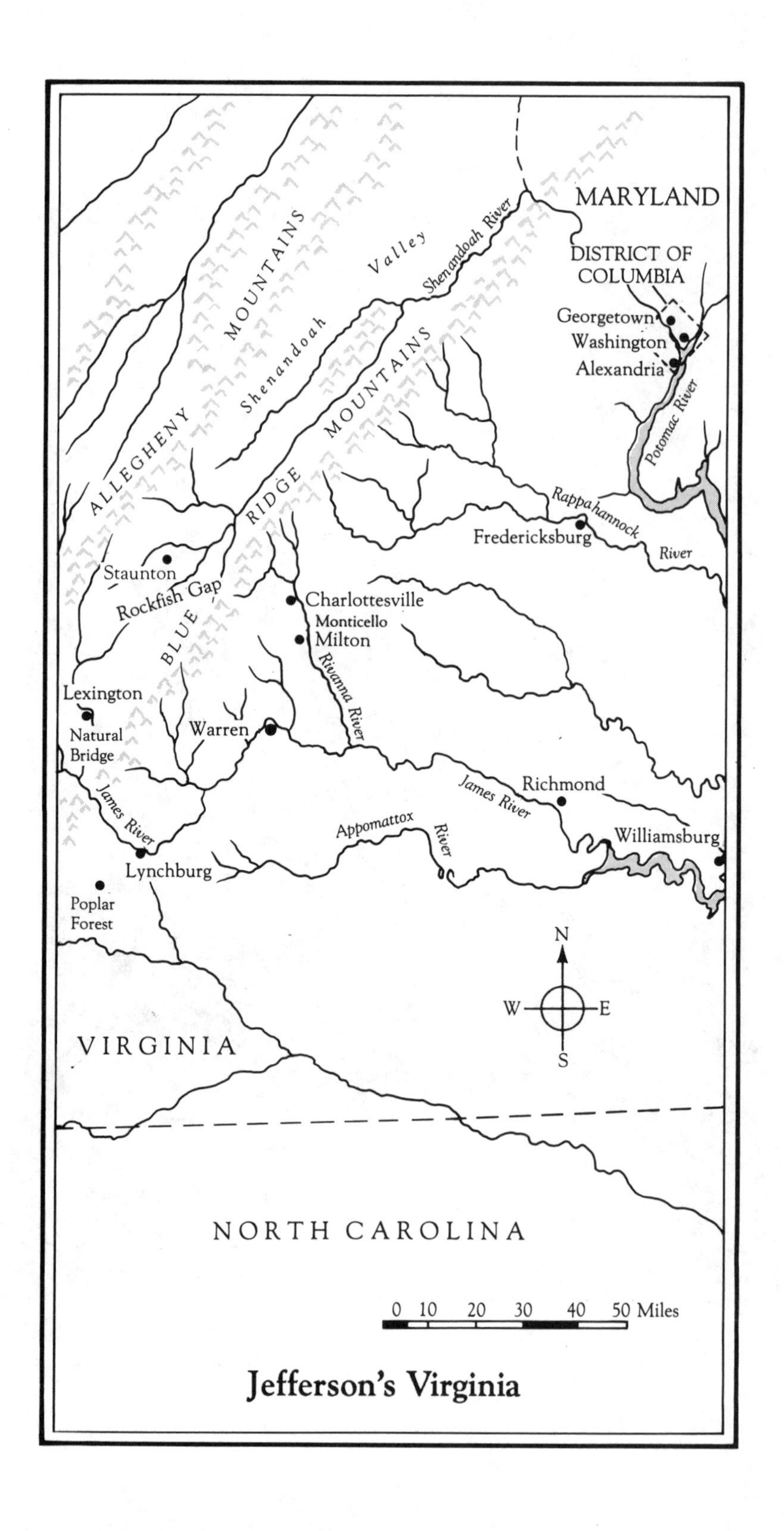

Jefferson's Virginia

Starting out rather small, says the historian Forrest McDonald, Peter Jefferson "carved out a vast estate by overawing and outwitting his peers, speculating in lands, persuading or killing Indians as the case required, marrying well, acquiring slaves, and otherwise living up to the mid-eighteenth-century Virginian's notion of manhood."

Peter's standing brought him the posts of justice of the peace, sheriff, and county surveyor. When he married Jane Randolph he gained a family connection far richer and more extensive than his own. The Randolphs were large landowners and slaveholders and their powerful clan was linked to just about every branch of the Virginia gentry. Peter took his nineteen-year-old wife to live at the plantation named Shadwell in what is now Albemarle County. It was wild and beautiful country, on the edge of the western frontier. Virginia settlements were widely scattered, with the tobacco plantations seated along the rivers, where ships could take on the crops for delivery to England. Peter planted tobacco, wheat, and corn. Shadwell, like every Virginia plantation, had to be self-sufficient. Everything the family and its slaves used had to be grown or made at home.

Thomas was the third child to be born to this couple; two daughters came before. When he was about three, the family moved to a large plantation called Tuckahoe. The reason: William Randolph, a close friend of Peter's, and one of the innumerable clan of Randolphs, had just died. His will made Peter executor of the estate and asked him to move into the thirty-five-room house on their tobacco plantation so he could help care for the estate and the orphaned children. By now there were five Jefferson and three Randolph children. While supervising the Randolph holdings Peter saw to it that an overseer and a gang of slaves cleared the forest from his own lands in Albemarle.

A tutor was hired to instruct the Randolph and Jefferson children. They met in a little house in the yard. What they learned we do not know, for Jefferson never set it down.

But it was from Peter that the boy Thomas probably learned most. His father's great strength must have impressed him. Everyone remembered the time Peter had taken two hogsheads of tobacco, each weighing a thousand pounds, and lifted them from their sides to stand upright. And the time he watched three slaves struggling vainly to tear down an old building by pulling on it with ropes. Telling them to step aside, he grabbed the ropes and pulled down the structure by himself.

Thomas's handwriting he probably copied from his father's for they were very alike. Early on, Peter taught his son to read, as well as to do arithmetic, for with so large a household to manage, his mother must have been too busy. At Tuckahoe the boy learned to read music and play the violin, as well as to dance. "Music is the favorite passion of my soul," he said. Peter may well have taken young Thomas on surveying trips nearby, to teach him the rudiments of the craft as well as the art of drafting, a skill Thomas would make good use of throughout life. Peter's handiness and his knowledge of tools became part of Thomas's heritage. Busy as the father was, he found time for reading. His small library, open to Thomas, held books on history, geography, astronomy, literature, and law.

While living at Tuckahoe, Peter was sent by the Crown into the wilderness with a large party to survey the disputed boundaries for a huge domain between the Potomac and the Rappahannock rivers. The long adventure was packed with perils and hardships that thrilled Thomas when his father returned home and spoke of them. The governor chose Peter to prepare for publication a map of Virginia drawn from his survey. It greatly extended the geographical knowledge of the region and was relied upon for many years.

Stories of the wilderness Peter explored surely excited the natural curiosity of a child about the mysteries of the world around him. Next door lay the frontier, abounding in fierce animals, tumultuous mountain rapids, dangerous swamps—and Indians. In imagination he must have reached out to those vast spaces where no whites had ever gone. Indians no longer lived near Shadwell or Tuckahoe, but from his father Tom heard many stories of peaceful meetings with them, when surveys took Peter into the wilderness. Once in a while Indians would come by Shadwell on their way to Williamsburg, Virginia's capital. Thomas never forgot these brief encounters as he systematically, in later life, accumulated all the information and materials he could acquire in an attempt to understand the culture of the Native Americans.

When Thomas was about nine, the Jeffersons moved back to Shadwell. This would be his home until he was twenty-seven. The plantation buildings stretched along a slope above the Rivanna where a water mill stood. The property ran to some 400 acres, but Peter soon acquired more and more land on both sides of the river (including the site of Monticello) until he owned 2,650 acres. Two daughters were born here and then a son, the tenth and last of the family.

What did Thomas look like? There are no early portraits to tell us. But what some said of the young Jefferson has come down to us. He was quite tall for his age, skinny, awkward in movement, with big hands and feet. His eyes were hazel-blue, his hair a bright red, his skin freckled and easily sunburned. From his mother's side he took the aristocratic style and taste, its pride (its arrogance too), and its lavish generosity. From the yeomanry of his father's line came his great energy, his independent spirit, and the readiness to take advantage of any opening.

On their return to Shadwell, Peter decided to send Thomas to a Latin school taught by a Scotsman, the Reverend William Douglas. The boy boarded at the clergyman's house during school term and went back to Shadwell on vacations. During his five years with Douglas he learned the basics of Latin, Greek, and French but thought little of the man as a teacher. He was probably unhappy much of this

The view Jefferson saw looking north from Monticello. This picture was painted in the 1820s by Jane Bradick.

time, away from home for long school sessions and bored by a dull teacher. But on vacation he learned how to ride from his father, and how to hunt and take care of himself in the forest. He loved to walk in the woods and to climb the rocky hills.

By now Thomas was old enough to be taught the operation of a plantation. Peter instilled the responsibilities of a landowner and a slaveholder—the need for self-reliance and authority, for timeliness and precision in carrying out duties. He learned how to keep the books for a plantation, and watched his father teach slaves the skills of carpentry, milling and planting. Long after, Jefferson sent a young boy named after him ten practical rules of behavior, a decalogue he must have learned from his father:

1. Never put off until tomorrow what you can do today.
2. Never trouble another for what you can do yourself.
3. Never spend your money before you have it.
4. Never buy what you do not want, because it is cheap; it will be dear to you.
5. Pride costs us more than hunger, thirst and cold.
6. We never repent for having eaten too little.
7. Nothing is troublesome that we do willingly.
8. How much pain has cost us the evils which have never happened!
9. Take things always by their smooth handle.
10. When angry count ten, before you speak; if very angry one hundred.

During these years Peter greatly enlarged the plantation home at Shadwell and added several outbuildings. Then, in the summer of 1757, only forty-nine, he fell ill and died. His passing was a terrible blow to everyone, especially Thomas. The boy was far more devoted to his father than to his mother.

She bore Peter ten children; two of them died in infancy. She would survive her husband by nineteen years, giving her whole life to rearing the large family. Oddly, Jefferson never mentions her in his papers, and rarely even in his account books. It seems unlikely mother and son were ever close.

Now, at least in name, Thomas as the eldest male was suddenly the head of a large household. Under his care would come his mother, six sisters, and a little brother. How could he take care of so heavy a burden? It would be an especially difficult task because none of the Jefferson children were anywhere near him in intelligence, except Jane, who died in her mid-twenties. Two sisters and his brother were retarded. And this even though Jefferson's mother and father were not blood relations. By some oddity of inheritance Thomas had all the brilliance that might have fallen to his sisters and brother.

Peter's will divided his considerable property among his survivors. The estate's inventory shows he had more than sixty slaves, twenty-five horses, seventy head of cattle, and two hundred hogs. At twenty-one, Thomas would receive a share of the family lands, the livestock, and slaves. One of the slaves, named Sawny, was given to him now, to be his personal valet, together with Peter's books, maps, mathematical and surveying instruments, and his cherrywood desk and bookcase.

Named as Thomas's guardian was Dr. Thomas Walker—a prominent planter, surveyor, soldier, and politician—and three other men. They decided to send Thomas to the best school in the province, run by the Reverend James Maury. It was a log house about 12 miles from Shadwell. Thomas stayed there weekdays, came home weekends. He made friends with Maury's eight children, especially two of the boys, James, Jr., and Matthew.

Maury had a large library for that time, some 400 books covering many fields of knowledge. One of the colony's best-educated men, he was much admired by Thomas. In his two years with Maury the boy learned to read Greek and Roman authors in the original, a practice he would always maintain, and to range over current English literature as well as the classics. Himself a fine stylist, Maury pressed his pupils to master the English language. (Jefferson would show early on a talent for eloquence few in the colonies could match.) The boy's interest in the world of nature was intensified by Maury, who collected fossils and minerals from the region lying beyond the forests of the Piedmont encircling Albemarle County.

One of his schoolmates, James Maury, Jr., later recalled that Jefferson had been the outstanding scholar in his father's school. But he was painfully shy and would often get others to start projects he desired rather than to take the initiative himself. In so small a school there was little chance for community life. Thomas found his closest friend in Dabney Carr, a boy his own age, and they were much together both at school and away, riding their horses and roaming the woods.

The two years at Maury's school over, and nearly seventeen, Thomas was ready for college. There were few colleges to choose among. The New England schools were ruled out: they were too distant, the cost would be too high, and worse, he might develop a view of life totally alien to a Virginian of his class. Some planters' sons went to England for higher education, but the expense ruled that out. So the only place left was the College of William and Mary, the South's sole academic institution.

★ 2 ★

LEARNING THE LAW

It was in the early spring of 1760 that seventeen-year-old Thomas Jefferson arrived at Williamsburg to enter the College of William and Mary. Named for the British monarchs who had founded it with a grant in 1693, it was a small college of about 100 students and seven teachers. It had four branches: a grammar school for boys up to fifteen, a school of philosophy, a postgraduate divinity school, and a separate school for the few Indians who came. The philosophy department, which Jefferson entered, had two professors. One taught math, physics, and philosophy, the other rhetoric, logic, and ethics.

Faculty members were not allowed to marry and had to live on campus. Students could not marry either, but could live on or off campus. They could not keep horses, gamble, enter the pubs, or leave the campus without permission. Lying, cursing, drinking, quarreling, or fighting were forbidden. Yet in Thomas's time, many students kept guns and dogs in their dormitory rooms and stabled their horses in town, as any Southern gentleman would.

The Capitol of the Virginia colony in Williamsburg, as it looked when Jefferson was a student at the College of William and Mary

The College of William and Mary,
when Jefferson enrolled in 1760

His first view of Williamsburg must have excited Thomas. Never before had he seen a community with more than twenty houses. Here was the capital of Britain's largest colony, with 300 houses and 2,000 people, including slaves. In the months when the legislature met and the court sat, the place swarmed with country gentry here to do business and be entertained. After growing up in the wilderness, he found it a rare pleasure to be able to walk crowded streets, enter shops to buy whatever he liked, and enjoy plays and concerts.

He could watch the colony's leaders participating in the Capitol or roistering in the Raleigh Tavern. Through his mother he was kin to some of them and probably was invited to their social evenings. Ignoring the college rule, he kept a horse in town and on weekends took exploratory rides into the country. He played his violin in his dormitory room for his own pleasure, and tried to walk at least a mile every evening. Never a smoker, he enjoyed a good digestion and could eat almost anything.

He soon found the college disappointing. It was poorly governed and many of the faculty were ill prepared to teach. Too many students were there only because their wealthy families had forced them to come. They cared nothing for learning, and spent the two years drinking, gambling, and racing horses. The college rules were a joke to them, for the bumbling administration was unable to enforce discipline on either students or faculty.

Thomas took comfort from his circle of friends, including two he knew from Maury's school—John Walker and Dabney Carr—and a new one, John Page, the talented son of a wealthy planter, who would be like a brother to him for half a century. Later Carr would marry Jefferson's sister Martha. He met Patrick Henry too, an unpredictable young buck seven years his senior, in town to acquire a license to practice law after studying it for only six weeks. Patrick wore hunting clothes and a dirty shirt and chewed tobacco. He was the kind of "man's man" other men envied and girls were said to adore, but whom Jefferson came to detest. Perhaps because he was nothing like him.

The most important friend Thomas made was William Small of Scotland, who was some eight years older, an Oxford graduate recently appointed to fill a vacancy in the philosophy school. Small found Thomas to be that rare student, self-disciplined and devoted to study. Thomas enjoyed Small's free-ranging mind; he was the only professor who was not an Anglican clergyman. Many years later Jefferson told what Small meant to him:

> It was my great good fortune and what probably fixed the destinies of my life that Dr. William Small was then professor of mathematics, a man profound in most of the useful branches of science, with a happy talent of communication, correct and gentlemanly manners, and an enlarged and liberal mind. He, most happily for me, became soon attached to me and made me his daily companion when not engaged in the school; and from his conversation I got my first views of the expanse of science and of the system of things in which we are placed.

Small changed the way students were taught by introducing the lecture system, recently practiced in England and abroad. The old way was reliance on pure memory, with students reciting canned answers to questions the teachers pulled out of the textbooks. Small exposed his students to a much wider range of subjects and sources than they had known. Jefferson especially loved the study of mathematics, which Small called the queen of the sciences. On weekends the two would go on long walks together. Small's conversation opened Jefferson's mind to new concepts in science and philosophy, while he taught his prize student how to observe the living world of nature with fresh eyes.

Delighting in his young pupil, Small introduced Thomas to his own circle of friends. One was the lawyer George Wythe, and another the province's lieutenant governor, Francis Fauquier, a fine scholar and great patron of learning. They did not mind that the brilliant student was much younger than they. Besides, Thomas's ability to play the violin was put to happy use at the weekly musical parties the governor held in the palace. Here Thomas heard his first concert music, a pleasure he would introduce years later at Monticello.

From Fauquier, Thomas could borrow recent works of French and English literature, and at Fauquier's table pick up news of important happenings in England. Both Fauquier and Wythe had a strong interest in science, and Thomas probably took part in experiments they performed with Fauquier's scientific instruments and apparatus. He observed too how Fauquier kept a daily record of temperature, winds, and rainfall, a practice that may have led Jefferson to begin making his own records of the weather. Sitting at Fauquier's table with Wythe and Small, Thomas said later, he "heard more good sense, more rational and philosophical conversations, than in all my life besides."

With Wythe, reputed to be the best Greek and Latin scholar in Virginia, Thomas shared a love for the classics. The lawyer liked Thomas as much as Small did, and often had him to dinner. The guests thought Jefferson very attractive. Now 6 feet, 2 inches, he seemed even taller because of the way he held his slim body erect. In company he was cheerful, frank, and an entertaining talker. As a talented musician, dancer, and rider, he was welcome anywhere. Almost at once he became a favorite of the governor's palace circle.

The college years could be summed up by saying that what Thomas learned best came from the lectures of his beloved teacher, William Small, and his private conversations with Small, in whom he had found another father. Small left Williamsburg after six years and returned to England. His influence created in the college a liberal spirit of inquiry that helped point it in a new direction. As for Thomas, the habit he formed of serious study served him all his life. He detested the indolent habits of his fellow aristocrats. During his college years, tradition says, he studied fifteen hours a day and even on vacation spent most of his time with his books. "Determine never to be idle," he would advise his own children. "It is wonderful how much may be done if we are always doing." Luckily, he proved healthy enough to endure the self-imposed strains. He used to bathe his feet in cold water every morning and credited that habit with keeping him free of colds or fevers.

As Thomas neared the close of his college years, the question of what career to pursue troubled him. Students had far fewer choices then than now. Would it be medicine? Law? The ministry? Politics? Those were the major professions. Some went into the military, a career Thomas had no interest in. Trade? But commerce was controlled by Britain, the mother country. And as for manufacturing, there was almost none of it in the colonies.

Think seriously about the law, advised William Small. And when George Wythe offered Thomas the chance to study law in his office, he accepted it. He wasn't sure this promised a fulfilling life, but at least what he might learn should be useful in many other ways. He could not expect to grow rich at law. Still, as a landowner he could count on income from his acres.

There were no law schools in the colonies; they would not develop till after the Revolution. Generally, it was an apprentice system that legal hopefuls followed, but a system much less strict than the code that bound beginners through contracts to master craftsmen. At nineteen, Jefferson began to read law in Wythe's office. He could not have found a better model to follow, for though only thirty-five, Wythe was already one of Virginia's best lawyers. What he got from Wythe was guidance in what books to read and in what order to read them. No doubt Wythe had him look up cases in the Capitol's law library and to learn what he could by attending sessions of the General Court. He would be asked to do clerical tasks and to draw up legal papers, a service he performed clearly and carefully.

From what Jefferson later advised other young law students to do, we can assume he worked at his heavy volumes of law from eight to twelve each morning, because those were the peak hours of his energy. Afternoons he read in related fields—ethics, politics, history—and took time out for exercise. Evenings he gave to literature and oratory.

Even with so strict a program, he found time for fun. He went riding and was often seen at balls and parties given in the town. He met sixteen-year-old Rebecca Burwell at one of these and danced minuets with her. He seems to have fallen hard, but his shyness kept him from advancing his suit. Alone with her, his fluency fled and he would begin to stammer. Not long after, she married someone else. Jefferson moaned over his loss, but in time the painful feeling faded.

Jefferson spent five years reading law under Wythe. He believed he could do better learning law from books than from practice. Lawyers were too apt to unload their own boring business on apprentices, leaving them little time to study. Although books on law were far fewer then, the volumes at

George Wythe, with whom Jefferson studied law

hand were dense and difficult, lacking the order and lucidity that would begin to appear later, in Blackstone's famous *Commentaries.* Jefferson's habit was to make notes on his legal reading in a commonplace book, one he might wish to refer to later, just as he did when reading literature or history. He selected the most significant parts, condensed them, and added his own thoughts. His abstracts, which survive, show the value he placed on the case method of studying law.

While still in Wythe's office, Jefferson came of age and received his inheritance. His new family responsibilities obliged him to make long and frequent visits to Shadwell. That home would not be his until after his mother's death. But now, at twenty-one, he was the owner of around 5,000 acres and twenty-two slaves. He took on the active management of his property, renting his mother's 400 acres at Shadwell and hiring her slaves to join his in working the fields. He sold some land to get necessary cash, and from time to time would buy and sell other tracts. Over the years his holdings increased in size. That he continued to study law in Williamsburg, despite his huge inheritance, shows his aim in life was to be something more than a planter. Yes, he loved the Albermarle country, but his years in Williamsburg had opened up to him a much larger world.

It was while Jefferson was learning to be a lawyer that the differences between the American colonies and the mother country began to threaten what had been a peaceful, if rivalrous, connection. In 1763, when the French and Indian War ended in a British victory, vast territories were added to the Empire. Disputes with the colonies arose over how and when to settle the new lands, over the payment of war debts, over the right of the colonists to sell their raw materials to whomever they pleased. And most importantly, over their right to make their own decisions. How much power should Parliament have over policy in America? Why should the colonies have no voice in Parliament? Resentment grew over the way Parliament was directing colonial affairs. When money issues were mixed with political issues, the quarrel became harsher. In 1764 Parliament's Sugar Act taxed or restricted colonial products to the point where the Americans cried out it would ruin their economy. Then came the order obliging the Americans to provide barracks and supplies for the British troops.

And worse: the Stamp Act, placing a direct tax upon dozens of things the colonists used and needed. The measure fueled the fires of protest. Jefferson, always interested in what the legislature was doing, was standing at the door of the House that day in May of 1765 when Patrick Henry, newly elected to that body by the frontier people, took the floor to claim that no one but the assembly had the right to lay taxes upon the colony. He linked the name of King George III with that of Julius Caesar and Charles I, both of whom had been killed for being tyrants. As shouts of "Treason!" went up, Henry cried out, "If this be treason, make the most of it!" When Henry's resolutions against the tax were published, they ignited debate countrywide, and other colonies soon followed Virginia's lead.

The power of Henry's oratory to stir patriotic emotion for the resistance movement deeply impressed Jefferson. It was a skill he would never acquire himself. His eloquence would be expressed through the written, not the spoken, word. While he scorned Henry's intellectual laziness and his coarse manners, he recognized his native genius and his sensitivity to the feelings of the frontier people from whom he sprang. Jefferson's mentor, George Wythe, had earlier drafted strong statements for the assembly, calling on Britain to let the colonies tax themselves. London had ignored them. But king and Parliament could not be deaf to Patrick Henry's voice. He had sounded the alarm bell of the American Revolution. And Jefferson was there to hear it.

★ 3 ★

SPICE OF AMBITION

Not until he was twenty-three did Jefferson set foot outside Virginia. He wanted to see how other people lived, and since this would be his last summer vacation as a law student, it was a good time to go. In May 1766 he headed northward in a one-horse carriage driven by one of his young slaves. In Annapolis, Maryland's capital, he watched the legislature in action and joined in the public celebration of the repeal of the Stamp Act. Taking Virginia's lead, nine of the colonies had met in New York to threaten Britain with a boycott of her goods unless the tax bills were killed. Parliament backed down and repealed the Stamp Act.

Reaching Philadelphia, he was amazed at the city's size: 20,000 people, against Williamsburg's 2,000! Here he was inoculated against smallpox, one of the aims of his journey. Appalling outbreaks of the disease had occurred often in the colonies. Everyone was afraid of being blinded or crippled by it. Curious about the new inoculation, Jefferson decided to take his chances, although he had heard the crude method in use often did more harm than good. He was lucky. It would be some time before Jenner's superior vaccination was developed.

Going on to New York he found the town smaller than Philadelphia, and less appealing. He returned to Virginia by boat, reaching home after being away three months.

It was around this time that Jefferson began keeping records of many kinds. He took to carrying a pocket-sized memorandum book in which he jotted down notes on his personal expenses and property finances as well as odds and ends on people he met, books he read, things he observed. He wasn't wasting time; he expected all this information to prove useful. Later when he traveled, he would end each day by making notes. In the memo books as well as in a Garden Book he soon began, he recorded and analyzed the time and motion of his own and others' activities. Like a modern efficiency expert he figured out how to save time and labor.

It was this intense curiosity combined with social concern that earlier (when he was only twenty-two) had led him to initiate a proposal to clear the Rivanna River of obstructions to make it navigable. From a canoe he surveyed the river, calculating a 22-mile stretch could be cleared at reasonable cost. He got a neighboring legislator to induce the Burgesses to authorize the clearing of the Rivanna and two other rivers by private funding. Within five years the work was done, and the waters made useful passages for farm products and other goods.

In his Garden Book Jefferson recorded the planting and sowing of flowers and vegetables, trees and shrubs, a practice he would continue for over fifty years. It was an early sign of understanding how important statistics can be in public as well as private affairs.

Still another kind of record he maintained covered his reading. He copied out from the books he liked passages that intrigued him. We know what pleasure the works of Shakespeare, Molière, Cervantes and the old English ballads gave him. In Williamsburg he dropped in at the *Virginia Gazette,* whose publisher made money by importing books from England for his customers. Jefferson bought volumes for the personal library he had begun to build.

Language, his own and any other, fascinated him. Much later, in a letter to a friend, he said, "To read the Latin and Greek authors in their original is a sublime luxury, and I deem luxury in science to be at least as justifiable as in architecture, painting, gardening, or the other arts. I enjoy Homer in his own language infinitely beyond Pope's translation of him . . . it is an innocent enjoyment. I thank on my knees him who directed my early education for having put into my possession this rich source of delight . . ."

He began to perfect his French while studying law, and then taught himself Italian, reading such authors as Machiavelli. He was one of the first people in America or England to study the Anglo-Saxon language, thinking it useful in his profession because many legal terms came from that language. He traced thousands of English words to their ancient roots in Old English, and arranged them alphabetically to create the first Anglo-Saxon dictionary.

In his diverse interests and his openness to new ideas Jefferson was an example of the free-ranging mind shaped by the Enlightenment. This was the term given to the main trend of thought in his time. In England and France, thinkers like Newton, Bacon, Locke, and Descartes had developed a rational approach to social, political, economic, and religious questions. They did not agree on all things, but underlying their ideas was a basic principle: that the world was governed by the laws of nature, and that the mind, or reason, could understand and master those laws.

But to do so, the mind must be free—free of dogmatism, religious intolerance, censorship, free of the tyranny of the church, the state, the academy, free to follow the teachings of science and reason wherever they led. These thinkers believed that society had an obligation to advance the hap-

1774

May. 4. the blue ridge of mountains covered with snow.

5 a frost which destroyed almost every thing. it killed the wheat, rye, corn, many tobacco plants, and even large saplings. the leaves of the trees were entirely killed. all the shoots of vines. at Monticello near half the fruit of every kind was killed; and before this no instance had ever occurred of any fruit killed here by the frost. in all other places in the neighborhood the destruction of fruit was total. this frost was general & equally destructive thro the whole country and the neighboring colonies.

14. cherries ripe.

16. first dish of pease from earliest patch.

26. a second patch of peas come to table.

June. 4. Windsor beans come to table.

5. a third & fourth patch of peas come to table.

13. a fifth patch of peas come in.

July. 13. last dish of peas.

18. last lettuce from Gehee's

23. Cucumbers from our garden.

31. Watermelons from our patch.

Aug. 3. Indian corn comes to table.

Black-eyed peas come to table

Nov. 16. this morning the Northern part of the Blue ridge is white with snow.

17. the first frost sufficient to kill any thing.

English	fog	rain	snow
French	brouillard	pluie	neige
Delaware	ääuän	suuklan	uüna
Unami	....	sù-ke-laan	guun
Monsi	....	sù-ke-laan	guun
Chippewa	....	ke-me-wàn	ac-guun
Knistenaux	pakishikow	kimiwoin	counah
Algonquin	awinni	ki mi woini	so qui po
Tawa	....	ki-mi-wàn	ac-guun
Shawanee	....	ke-me-wàni kimmawane	[illegible] coone
Nanticoke	hou,e,wen	uineeou sù-k[illegible]an	quō-no guun
Mohiccan	....	sokandan so-ke-[illegible]an	washaná wa-scha-ni
Unquachog	....	sùkenun	soáctpo
Oneida	täahwanläeh	yocomoal	onaieghta
Cayuga	....	....	....
Onondaga	ojinquara täawenohhu	ne-jòhhtarònti	ogéra
Miami	.... uoonuch	petitènivé petitanuch	monètwa monatuch
Cherokee	.... [illegible]	oc, caiu, cuh. kawshah [illegible]	ainhecha. ainochah [illegible]
Chickasaw	ooktoolidge	oo,buh. oombah	ookte.
Choctaw	tobe.	oombuh. oomboh	ooktoo,sau. sokootooshé.
Creek	o,pilthle	ooske	e,toote thluc,co
Tuscarora	....	....	....
Chetimacha	chitoe	haya	naetspechapechnicha
Atacapa	shy combnst	caucau	adlesht

A page from Jefferson's Garden Book, recording a killing frost on May 5, 1774; and a page on comparative vocabulary from his study of Native American languages iness of its people. They were committed to do away with inhuman penal codes and with torture, to improve the lives of the poor, to end the slave trade and slavery itself.

How could this be done? Our innate ability to reason, they said, would guide us to the means by which we could form a more perfect society. The movement was given powerful impetus by a book called *Essay Concerning Human Understanding.* It was written in the seventeenth century by John Locke, an English philosopher, at a time when the English were rebelling against the tyrannical rule of Charles I and setting up parliamentary government. The English rebels, fighting for representative government, opened up discussion of democracy. Locke asserted that happiness is what all people desire, and that in the long run private happiness and public good would coincide.

As a political thinker, Locke believed that in the original state of nature people were happy. All were equal and independent; none had a right to harm another in his or her "life, health, liberty or possessions." He held the right of property to be important because each of us has a right to the products of his own labor. In his view revolution in some circumstances was not only a right but an obligation. If political authority was legitimate and just, he opposed revolution. But where government was tyrannical, he advocated effective protest.

Like Locke, Jefferson believed the human mind might not be able to know everything, but we could at least try to master whatever concerned our conduct. To doubt, to question, was a good habit of mind. And the power of reason, Jefferson said, "must be our last judge and guide in everything."

Locke's was a practical philosophy, anchored in human experience. His ideas were in the air that the Founding Fathers breathed. They found their earliest American advocate in Benjamin Franklin, and then in Jefferson, who gave the most brilliant expression to them. Most likely, it was at Governor Fauquier's table, where Jefferson often sat with his friends Wythe and Small, that his receptive mind first absorbed the warm and moving ideas of the Enlightenment.

After three years of legal studies, Jefferson began to practice law. He had much business in the county courts, to which he rode on horseback, accompanied by his slave Jupiter, who carried his luggage in a cart. They stayed in whatever lodgings were available. These journeys into the rural districts brought the young lawyer together with farmers who flocked into the small towns on court days. They came not only on legal business but to trade horses, buy and sell slaves, auction property, collect or pay debts, and provide the family some fun. Roving entertainers put on street shows, and peddlers hawked their wares.

The magistrates were not trained jurists but prominent local citizens. So too were the judges who sat on the General Court in Williamsburg. It was wealth and social standing that elevated them to the bench, not legal knowledge.

Jefferson's practice was the routine business of drawing up deeds and wills, serving as executor, guardian, or witness, dealing with land claims, debts, the recovery of slaves, slander, assault and battery. He never was involved in sensational trials, and in contrast to Abraham Lincoln there are few amusing anecdotes about his life on the circuit. Unlike Patrick Henry he built no reputation for emotional appeals to the jury. He spoke in court with ease, but always from notes, and could not raise his voice for long without growing hoarse.

His practice grew so steadily that by the end of his seven years at law he had recorded acting as counsel in about a thousand cases. Was it a profitable profession for him? His fees would have added up to a decent income—if he had been able to collect everything due him. His records show he never got as much as half what was owed. Most lawyers of his time had the same complaint. Still, considering the living his estates provided, the defaults could not ruin him.

It was almost inevitable that he became involved in politics. Everyone was a gentleman in his crowd; to gain distinction you had to win leadership in public affairs. In 1768 he was elected one of Albemarle's two burgesses. The campaign took minimal effort and expense. For one thing, not many people were eligible to vote. You had to own at least 50 unsettled acres, or 25 if you had a plantation with a house. Women, blacks, Indians, and the poor had no vote. Those who did cast a ballot did it openly; there was no secret ballot. Usually the vote went the way the county leaders wanted it to go.

If any public issues were debated, there is no record of it. The candidates were expected to provide the freeholders with rum or punch and cakes. The reserved Jefferson was polite to all, but he was no backslapper or crowd-pleaser. Luckily, to the Virginia gentlemen who ran the show it did not matter. It seems ironic that in the years ahead Jefferson would become the hero of the plain people.

Did he have an appetite for politicking? He always claimed he disliked it, yet he never avoided it. He admitted a "little spice of ambition," and like any other young man he wanted to be honored. The colony's leaders could see early on that this was a young man of great talent and energy. For the next fifteen years he would serve in the legislature, taking care of its business while practicing law and managing his farms.

It was just before his election to the legislature that Jefferson attempted an "affair" with Betsey Walker, the wife of a neighbor. John Walker, his friend from boyhood, was away from home for some months, attending an Indian conference in Albany. He had asked Jefferson to look after his wife and baby daughter. With the husband gone, Jefferson wrote love notes to Mrs. Walker, suggesting there would be no harm in a little lovemaking among friends. On one occasion he was said to have gone into her bedroom, prepared to take her by force, but she had resisted, threatening him with a pair of scissors.

Not until many years later did Walker learn of his friend's disloyalty. At that time, when Walker said he wanted to make Jefferson the executor of his will, Mrs. Walker told her astonished husband that Jefferson was no true friend, and told him why. Satisfied that his wife was innocent, Walker did nothing. Jefferson was far off in Paris then, serving America as minister to France. Neither man wanted to make the story public. Many years later, however, the story broke in the news and, as we shall see, became a political weapon against President Jefferson.

★ 4 ★

MARTHA, MONTICELLO —AND REVOLUTION

The year Jefferson became a legislator he began to build a home at Monticello. The site was a "low mountain"—*monticello* in Italian—across the Rivanna from Shadwell. Slave laborers had leveled off the top of the mountain and now they began to dig the cellar for the first of the two small pavilions that would flank the main house.

Architecture was one of Jefferson's earliest passions, and this was the wealthy amateur's chance to create something extraordinary, something beautiful, a kind of Eden to suit his own tastes and needs. His ideas about design and building came from reading and observation. He had watched his father enlarge Shadwell and had begun to collect an architectural library. His was not simply a gentleman's fancy, but a burning desire to make a great and original building himself, to create out of brick and mortar a practical and handsome structure.

His early drawings for Monticello show the influence of European studies of architecture, one of which introduced him to the work of Palladio. The Italian master's designs so delighted him that he added octagonal bays to the parlor and

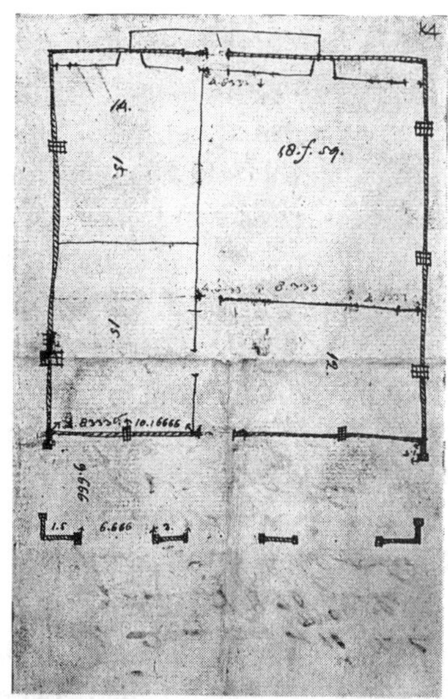

Jefferson's earliest sketch for a square, wooden, four-room house at Monticello

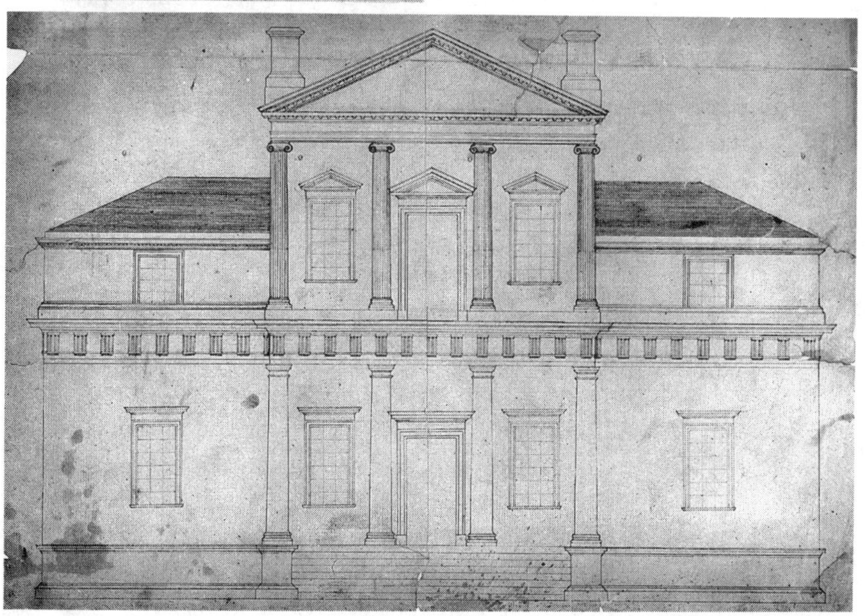

Jefferson's elevation drawing for the house as it took on grander proportions

the ends of the new house, and applied the same shape to his garden as well.

One of his innovations was to place under one roof the many diverse service units that a plantation needed. The outbuildings for kitchen, laundry, woodshed, storage bins scattered about the typical Virginia manor, he designed for the main house, on the basement level, opening on one side to ground level, and covered with terraces. It was another idea he took from Palladio.

The making of Monticello would become Jefferson's lifetime avocation. Always thinking about designs for additions or changes, he created some 500 drawings all told. The experts call him the first American to make working drawings as well as architectural designs. His achievement earned him a rating as America's "first great native-born architect."

One day in February 1770, while Jefferson was away, the house at Shadwell burned to the ground. Neither his mother nor the children were injured, but most of his papers and books were destroyed. All that was saved were his violin and several beds. The family moved into another building on the plantation while the house was rebuilt. In a few years Jefferson managed to assemble another collection of more than 1,200 books as well as some scientific instruments.

The house at Monticello was scarcely begun when Shadwell went up in flames. But by November 1770 Jefferson was able to move into the one completed room. Progress in building was painfully slow. He could supervise construction only on periodic visits while carrying on his law practice and legislative duties. He had to wrestle with the practical problems of building and maintaining a road up to the mountaintop, of carting tools and materials up to it, of making the brick on the site, of finding space to store materials. He relied almost exclusively on his black carpenters, joiners, blacksmiths and painters, taught by whites who were occasionally still called in. Finding solutions to water shortages and soil erosion added to his troubles. But he pushed on relentlessly, grafting his first trees, sowing clover for the fields and grass for the lawn.

The Great House Jefferson envisioned was still rather rare in Virginia. Most whites and blacks lived in one- or two-room wooden houses with crude lofts, wooden chimneys, and earthen or wooden floors. Not until his time did more upper-class whites begin to move into larger and more permanent quarters. Jefferson formed a deep, almost mystical attachment to his Monticello. "I am happy nowhere else, and in no other society," he would write later. His plantation and gardens were in stark contrast to the common run of Virginia farms, where disorder seemed to reign.

That fall of 1770, as Jefferson moved into his incomplete new house, he met the woman he would marry. She was Martha Wayles Skelton, a young widow, and the eldest daughter of John Wayles, a wealthy landowner, lawyer, and slave trader. At seventeen she had married Bathurst Skelton, who died in two years, leaving his nineteen-year-old widow and a small son, who soon died too.

Martha was a lovely woman, slight of figure, with fair complexion, auburn hair and large hazel eyes. Gay-spirited, she sang well, played the piano and harpsichord, and was a good conversationalist. So attractive, talented, and wealthy a widow had many suitors in her four years of widowhood, but none could compete with Jefferson. He went courting many times to the Wayles home, until Martha consented to marry him. The wedding took place on New Year's Day, 1772, at her home.

The couple planned to leave right after the ceremony, but a record snowfall delayed them for two weeks. It was late at night when they finally reached Monticello after a 100-mile journey in deep snow, only to find the slaves asleep and no food on hand, only a half bottle of wine. So toasting each other merrily, they started their new life in the only room finished, the 18-by-18-foot "Small House," as Jefferson called it, which later became part of the South Pavilion of the completed mansion. It was a single all-purpose room, under which there was a slave kitchen.

Jefferson stayed on with his bride until the spring, missing the legislative session and forgetting about his law practice. In September their first child was born. Named Martha, after her mother, she barely survived her first six months. But eventually she grew strong and was a joy to her father till the end of his days.

Mrs. Jefferson bore six children within ten years, five girls and one boy. Only two, Martha and Maria, would survive infancy. The one son died so quickly he was never given a name. Maria lived to be twenty-five. A short life was common in that century. Jefferson had already lost his oldest sister, Jane, when she was twenty-five. He missed her badly; she was his equal in many things and they had spent much time together. In May of 1773 he lost his best friend and brother-in-law, Dabney Carr, a promising young lawyer. He was buried in the Jefferson family plot at Monticello. A week later, rigidly sticking to his custom, Jefferson noted for the record the time it had taken to dig the grave, and then calculated how many acres one man could dig at that same rate. Jefferson kept close to his widowed sister and became a second father to her six children. Later, her family would move in with his.

Scarcely ten days after Carr's death, John Wayles, Martha's father, died. Jefferson was named an executor of the estate. When the property was divided, Martha's share was 11,000 acres and 135 slaves, which more than doubled Jefferson's holdings. Adding to his own fifty the slaves passed on to his wife, he now had a great abundance of "servants," as the planters preferred to call them. Among them were Betty Hemings and her family. She was the daughter of an English sea captain and an African slave woman. She bore fourteen children of many shades of color, most of whom would now serve Jefferson as slaves. Six of them were said in the Monticello slave quarters to have been fathered by the late John Wayles. If the story is correct, they were the half sisters and half brothers of Jefferson's wife.

Many slave owners made slave women their concubines; the children born of such unions were legally slaves and could be sold. Though the practice was widespread, planters almost never admitted to cohabiting with their slaves. They would say overseers or poor whites were the men responsible if any children were born.

As for Jefferson's wife, aristocrat though she was, her responsibility as mistress of the plantation demanded the most arduous work. She had to manage the domestic routine of a large household and the many guests who frequently dined and stayed with them. Meat, dairy, vegetables, fruits had to be gathered, stored, preserved, prepared, and served. There was bedding and clothing to be knitted or sewn; soap, candles, and dyes to be manufactured. She looked after the house slaves and the food, clothing, training, and medical care they needed.

Above all came childbearing. Out of the 120 months of her life with Jefferson, Martha was pregnant in fifty-four. Nursing, raising, and educating her children consumed still more of her time and energy. But this was not at all unusual. Their elder daughter, Martha, would bear twelve children, a birth rate equaled by many plantation wives of their day. Mrs. Jefferson, however, was physically not up to the demands of such a life.

Remember too, that all during their marriage she lived in a house only half-finished, with construction always going on, and noise, debris, dust, mud, and scaffolding making her surroundings painfully ugly. One wonders too why Jefferson, knowing his wife's health to be at serious risk, kept making her pregnant.

When Jefferson married into the Wayles family, taking his wife's inheritance of land and slaves, he put himself into a tangled network of racial and family relationships, holding his own wife's half sisters and half brothers in slavery. (How this would influence his views on race and slavery we will see later.)

With his property so vastly increased Jefferson had to expand his records. In 1774 he began his Farm Book. In it he noted his agricultural operations, data on plants he collected, calculations on how much food and clothing his slaves needed. Progress on Monticello continued: roads encircling the mountain, fruit trees planted, a vegetable garden laid out. When the Italian grape-grower Philip Mazzei moved to America to buy land and build a house nearby, Jefferson welcomed him as a friend, improved his own Italian, added Italian wines and vegetables to his table.

Meanwhile Jefferson had been serving in the House of Burgesses. As a better writer than most, he was given the job of drafting public papers while serving on various committees. He rarely spoke up during sessions of the House. Neither did George Washington, the member from Fairfax whom he met here for the first time. Surrounded by abler politicians, older and more distinguished than he, Jefferson learned much by observing them.

Things were quiet for a time, as British policy shifted, wavered. Then on March 5, 1770, British soldiers fired on a Boston crowd and five people fell dead, with many more wounded. After the Boston Massacre, petitions from the colonies flooded into London asking for settlement of colonial grievances. They were rejected. Committees of Correspondence were created in the colonies as networks for exchanging information and developing common actions. The colonists took to boycotting British tea in protest against the duty they had to pay for it. In Boston, late in 1773, patriots boarded three British ships and dumped their cargoes of tea into the harbor. That action infuriated the British government. It closed the port of Boston and imposed military rule on Massachusetts.

The other colonies rallied to Boston's aid. Virginia proposed they all meet to consider what to do next. In September 1774, fifty-six delegates gathered in Philadelphia and voted to shut off trade with Britain. No longer would the colonies be bound by Parliament's laws or the king's word when it infringed on their liberties. They demanded repeal of all the offensive acts passed by Parliament since 1763, and set a second Congress for the spring of 1775.

Jefferson had not been a leading figure in the early actions against Britain. But now he helped create Virginia's Committee of Correspondence and backed the idea of a general congress to promote the revolt against Parliament.

It was in the summer of 1774 that Jefferson made his first major literary contribution to the patriot cause. It happened when he and John Walker were chosen to represent Albemarle County in a convention to discuss the future of the colonies. Asked to prepare motions for the delegates to send to the First Continental Congress, Jefferson set down his ideas in the form of resolutions. An attack of dysentery disabled him on his way to Williamsburg and he had to return home. He sent on his draft, however, to the delegates who were to go to Philadelphia. Without consulting him, some of his friends meanwhile published the resolutions as a pamphlet called *A Summary View of the Rights of British America.* It was reprinted in Philadelphia and England, and although his name was not on it, everyone soon knew who the author was.

It was a closely reasoned, though angry statement of colonial grievances. It accused the British of not listening to the colonies, of cheating them, of being unfair, of punishing the innocent. It struck at the British view that the colonies were children who owed obedience and deference to the mother country. Americans did not wish to separate from Britain, Jefferson said. But if the government did not listen? It was a pamphlet that, as one historian wrote, "invited hanging" from Britons who considered such views traitorous.

But to radical Americans his fiery statement of principle made Jefferson a champion of freedom and self-government

Presented to Joseph C. Cabell

A

SUMMARY VIEW

OF THE

RIGHTS

OF

BRITISH AMERICA.

SET FORTH IN SOME

RESOLUTIONS

INTENDED FOR THE

INSPECTION

OF THE PRESENT

DELEGATES

OF THE

PEOPLE OF VIRGINIA.

NOW IN

CONVENTION.

BY A NATIVE, AND MEMBER OF THE HOUSE OF BURGESSES.

WILLIAMSBURG:

PRINTED BY CLEMENTINA RIND

1774.

The cover of Jefferson's first publication on behalf of the rebelling colonists who would concede nothing to Britain. The majority were not yet ready to go as far as he did. Two years later, however, when cascading events would propel them leftward, they would ask him to draft the Declaration of Independence.

Caught up in politics, Jefferson gave less and less time to his law practice. Finally, in August 1774, he decided to quit. The Wayles inheritance had multiplied his responsibilities at the same time that it made it unnecessary for him to supplement his income. Now he could take up law and government in their larger meaning—the natural rights of the individual and the legal rights of the colonies. He had come to see himself not only as a loyal Virginian but as an American who must stand firm with all his fellow Americans.

The tidal wave of change reached into every corner of the colonies. In March 1775 Jefferson was one of the Virginia burgesses who met in Richmond without Governor Dunmore's approval. He heard Patrick Henry cry out to the legislature, "We must fight! Is life so dear, or peace so sweet, as to be purchased at the price of chains and slavery? Forbid it, almighty God! I know not what course others may take, but as for me, give me liberty or give me death!"

For the first time in his public career Jefferson took the floor, to back Henry warmly. The assembly voted to get ready for war. A few weeks later came news that blood had been spilled in Massachusetts. A British general had sent a thousand soldiers to capture a store of munitions at Concord, hidden by farmers organized as Minutemen. They grabbed their guns and resisted the Redcoats. The American Revolution had begun.

When the news reached Virginia by express rider, weapons and powder were stored and men prepared to fight. Governor Dunmore fled to a British warship lying off Yorktown. He never went back to Williamsburg.

The Second Continental Congress, meeting in Philadelphia, now had a war on its hands. Plans were laid to raise an army, funds, and supplies. In June, Jefferson joined the delegates in Philadelphia as a substitute for Peyton Randolph, who was called home. This was his debut as a national figure. He was at the height of a prosperity he would never know again, and deeply satisfied in his role as husband and father. But his pleasure in private life and as a planter would never be foremost again. From now on, his fate would be inseparable from America's.

Jefferson had come to Philadelphia with two slaves and four horses. He lodged with a cabinetmaker and took meals at the fashionable City Tavern with other delegates. The town's shops were inviting; he bought books and music, living in patrician style in the midst of revolution.

Congressional sessions in the State House (later called Independence Hall) ran from 9 A.M. to late afternoon, and committee duties often held him evenings too. Debate and decision among the sixty-odd delegates was slow going, for any motion required unanimity. Jefferson was faithful to his duties, though silent in debate. In committee discussion, however, he was frank and decisive. While others shone as speakers, his recognized talent with the pen committed him to paperwork.

His first major assignment was to help redraft a manifesto on taking up arms. Through this committee he got to know both Benjamin Franklin, just back from England, and John Jay, with both of whom he would have a long relationship. A comparison of the two versions Jefferson penned shows how carefully he used language. He would set down alternative phrases and then cross out the less preferable ones. Though his final draft was watered down in committee, the call to take up arms proved quite popular. This and other documents he helped write for the Congress were needed to advance the patriot cause both at home and abroad. It was propaganda, of course, a weapon in the psychological warfare which he excelled in. As yet, and for some time to come, his rare eloquence would not be publicly recognized.

In August the Congress recessed and Jefferson went home. He bought a fine violin from one of the Randolph clan, John, who sided with Britain and decided to move there. In a letter to him Jefferson said he hoped Britain would be wise enough to soon put an end to "this unnatural contest." My first wish, he went on, "is a restoration of our just rights; my second, a return to the happy period, when, consistently with duty, I may withdraw myself totally from the public stage, and pass the rest of my days in domestic ease and tranquility, banishing every desire of ever hearing what passes in the world."

The prospects for peace were poor. The king had already proclaimed the colonies in a state of rebellion and was threatening drastic punishment for traitors.

It was soon after his arrival home that Jefferson's eighteen-month-old daughter, Jane, died. He stayed there a month, dealing with plantation affairs, then went back to Philadelphia. Congress was busy with the raising and supplying of the military, technical matters that bored him because he could be of little use. Saddened by the loss of Jane, he learned that his daughter Martha was ill. When his wife did not respond to his letters, he grew so anxious that in late December he rode home. He found his daughter still not well, but everything else seemed all right.

Soon after he arrived war actually began in Virginia. Lord Dunmore declared martial law, bombarded Norfolk, and called on the slaves to desert their masters and join the British. Jefferson's place was far from the coastal region where Dunmore operated, so the family was in no danger.

It was now that he read the strongest case for a total break with England. It was *Common Sense*, a powerful pamphlet by Thomas Paine. A poor English immigrant looking for a fresh start in life, Paine had settled in Philadelphia two years before. Siding with the radicals, he argued for immediate independence. His brilliant appeal sold 150,000 copies, a huge number for that time. Like Jefferson, he urged Americans not to look to authority: rely on "nothing more than the simple facts, plain argument, and common sense," he said, as he pointed out how ridiculous it was for a continent to belong to an island.

Jefferson was about to rejoin the Congress when, late in March, his mother had a stroke and died in an hour. Her death, about which he said nothing, forced him to stay longer than planned to handle the settlement of her estate. Perhaps this complex of misfortunes caused the prolonged migraine headache that attacked him. It was the first sign of a troubling condition that would recur for many years, usually when he was under stress. Not until May 1776 did it relent, and he was able to leave Monticello for Philadelphia.

★ 5 ★

WRITING THE DECLARATION

A heavy heat blanketed the town when he arrived. Jefferson moved away from the center in search of cooler air, renting a bedroom and parlor on the second floor of a new brick house at 7th and Market streets. It was owned by a newly wed bricklayer named Graff.

Word reached him that Virginia wanted her delegates to propose to Congress that the colonies declare themselves to be free and independent states. She declared her own independence, ran up a new flag over the Williamsburg capital, and set about drafting her own constitution.

Congress soon took up Virginia's challenge. On June 7 a Virginia delegate, Richard Henry Lee, introduced an independence resolution. The Congress began the debate; Jefferson was silent but took careful notes. Meanwhile a committee was appointed to draft a declaration of independence—just in case. Serving on it were John Adams, Benjamin Franklin, Roger Sherman, Robert Livingston, and Jefferson. Though only thirty-two, and one of the youngest men in Congress, he was a natural choice. The five men met at Franklin's home to agree upon the general form of the dec-

Jefferson as seen by a Swiss artist, Pierre Eugene Du Simitière. This was made the same year the thirty-two-year-old wrote the Declaration of Independence. The original rough draft of its first page is shown at right.

laration. They hoped it would generate large-scale support for independence. Then they asked Jefferson to write it. Why him? Partly because of his skill with the pen, and partly because they wanted Virginia, as the oldest, largest, and most committed of the states, to take the lead.

For seventeen days Jefferson worked on the draft in his parlor, sitting on a revolving Windsor chair while writing on the portable mahogany lap desk which a cabinetmaker had recently built from Jefferson's own drawing. He got up each day at dawn, soaked his feet in chilled water to protect against catching cold, and then went to his task. He looked at neither book nor pamphlet, he said long after. All the ideas in the Declaration rested on "the harmonizing sentiments of the day, whether expressed in conversation, in letters, printed essays, or in the elementary books of public rights . . ."

Long after, Jefferson told what he set out to do with the Declaration. It was to be an appeal to the public opinion of the whole world, an appeal to humanity's sense of justice.

A Declaration by the Representatives of the UNITED STATES OF AMERICA, in General Congress assembled.

When in the course of human events it becomes necessary for one people to dissolve the political bands which have connected them with another, and to assume among the powers of the earth the separate and equal station to which the laws of nature & of nature's god entitle them, a decent respect to the opinions of mankind requires that they should declare the causes which impel them to the separation.

We hold these truths to be self-evident; that all men are created equal; that they are endowed by their creator with [inherent &]inalienable rights; that among these are life, liberty, & the pursuit of happiness; that to secure these rights, governments are instituted among men, deriving their just powers from the consent of the governed; that whenever any form of government becomes destructive of these ends, it is the right of the people to alter or to abolish it, & to institute new government, laying it's foundation on such principles & organising it's powers in such form, as to them shall seem most likely to effect their safety & happiness. prudence indeed will dictate that governments long established should not be changed for light & transient causes: and accordingly all experience hath shewn that mankind are more disposed to suffer while evils are sufferable, than to right themselves by abolishing the forms to which they are accustomed. but when a long train of abuses & usurpations [begun at a distinguished period, &] pursuing invariably the same object, evinces a design to reduce them under absolute Despotism, it is their right, it is their duty, to throw off such government, & to provide new guards for their future security. such has been the patient sufferance of these colonies; & such is now the necessity which constrains them to [expunge] (alter) their former systems of government. the history of the present king of Great Britain is a history of [unremitting] (repeated) injuries and usurpations, [among which, appears no solitary fact to contradict the uniform tenor of the rest, but all have] in direct object the establishment of an absolute tyranny over these states. to prove this, let facts be submitted to a candid world, [for the truth of which we pledge a faith yet unsullied by falsehood.]

What he wrote was

> not to find out new principles, or new arguments, never before thought of; not merely to say things which had never been said before, but to place before mankind the common sense of the subject, in terms so plain and firm as to command their assent, and to justify ourselves in the independent stand we are compelled to take. Neither aiming at originality of principle or sentiment, nor yet copied from any particular and previous writing, it was intended to be an expression of the American mind, and to give to that expression the proper tone and spirit called for by the occasion.

Despite what he said fifty years later, he did take a good deal from another source—his own. The longest part of the Declaration—the list of the abuses by which Britain meant "to reduce the people under absolute despotism"—was adapted from a similar list of grievances Jefferson had put into his draft constitution for Virginia just a few weeks before. He also made use of a Declaration of Rights that George Mason had drafted for Virginia, which had adopted it before its constitution. All these ideas, as he said, were in the air; they were the mental fodder of the American patriots whose spirits he tried to voice.

But how did he put this into writing? Each thought, as it came to him, he jotted down on a separate sheet. Then he decided on the best way to tie them together, and finally, rewrote them in the form he wanted the committee to see. When he was done, he showed the draft to Adams and then to Franklin. They made minor changes, and the committee as a whole added a few more. Then it went to Congress, which tabled it until July 2 when it voted yes to independence. Now the delegates were ready to review Jefferson's draft. For three days, July 2–4, they discussed it while he writhed over the changes some asked for.

Like most writers, Jefferson was not happy over people tampering with his text. But historians agree that the changes made in his draft strengthen it. The biggest change, in order to gain unanimous acceptance in Congress, was to delete his attack upon George III for allowing the slave trade to continue. Jefferson had denounced the slave trade as a "cruel war against human nature itself." This cut was made, Jefferson said, upon the request of South Carolina and Georgia, "who had never attempted to restrain the importation of slaves, and who on the contrary wished to continue it. Our northern brethren also I believe felt a little tender under these censures, for though their people had very few slaves themselves yet they had been pretty considerable carriers of them to others." But while the king had blocked attempts to stop the slave trade, he was hardly to blame for slavery in the colonies.

On July 4 Jefferson woke early, recorded the temperature at 6 A.M. at 68 degrees, breakfasted, and stopped at a shop on Market Street to buy seven pairs of gloves for his wife. He was in his seat at nine when the Congress met. The Declaration was presented, and accepted without dissent. Now it had to be printed and copies rushed to the states. Probably Jefferson himself took his original copy to Dunlap, the printer for Congress, where it seems to have been cut into sections for distribution to several printers who set it in type. (That may explain why researchers have never been able to find the original copy.)

Philadelphia was naturally the first place to have the Declaration proclaimed. On July 8 a great crowd assembled in the State House yard shortly after noon. When the reading ended, the audience cheered, troops paraded, bells rang all day, and that evening a sign bearing the coat of arms of George III was burned.

The famous painting by John Trumbull of the signing of the Declaration of Independence. Made many years after the event, it shows Washington seated; before him stands Jefferson with the document in hand, and the drafting committee is around him.

The State House in Philadelphia where the Continental Congress met. Later it was called Independence Hall. It is now a national museum.

The next day, after Washington had the Declaration read to his troops in New York City, the crowd tore down the gilded statue of George III. In Baltimore they burned the king in effigy; in Savannah they made a show of burying him. Not until August 2 did most of the fifty-five delegates to Congress sign the official engrossed parchment copy.

Adoption of the Declaration was the greatest question that Americans ever decided. And it has become the most cherished document in our history. What exactly is in it? Everyone knows how it begins, with these ringing words of Jefferson:

> When in the course of human events it becomes necessary for one people to dissolve the political bonds which have connected them with one another, and to assume among the powers of the earth, the separate and equal station to which the laws of nature and nature's God entitle them, a decent respect to the opinions of mankind requires that they should declare the causes which impel them to the separation.

That first paragraph expresses the mind of the Enlightenment. It connects the American experience with the experience of people everywhere, not just at this moment of history but in every era. It is "the laws of nature and nature's God" which entitle Americans to take this action. And it is with concern for the opinion of all humanity that Americans declare their independence and give the grounds for it.

Then comes the first long sentence of Jefferson's next paragraph, which I set out in the form of a list, in the order he gave it:

> that all men are created equal,
>
> that they are endowed by their creator with certain unalienable rights,
>
> that among these are life, liberty, and the pursuit of happiness,
>
> that to secure these rights governments are instituted among men, deriving their just powers from the consent of the governed,
>
> that whenever any form of government becomes destructive of these ends, it is the right of the people to alter or to abolish it,
>
> and to institute new government, laying its foundation on such principles, and organizing its power in such forms, as to them shall seem most likely to effect their safety and happiness.

Why does the Declaration say "all *men* are created equal?" Probably not with the deliberate aim of implying women are not equal. In Jefferson's time women were simply not considered as worth including. Politically they were invisible. They did much of the family's and the community's work in the home, on the farm, in occupations like midwifery, but they were just ignored when it came to political rights or civil equality. Abigail Adams, the wife of John Adams, one of the signers, reminded him of this when she wrote him, "I cannot say that I think you are very generous to the ladies for, whilst you are proclaiming peace and goodwill to men, emancipating all nations, you insist upon retaining an absolute power over your wives."

Which people were entitled to the "unalienable rights" of "life, liberty, and the pursuit of happiness"? Not women, and not slaves or Native Americans, as we've seen. But it does no good to denounce the signers of the Declaration for holding the ideas of the privileged white men of their time. It is an unfair and fruitless moral burden to lay on those people centuries later. The point is to try to understand the conflicts of interest that lay behind their omission of large parts of humankind.

By using sweeping and inspirational language the Founding Fathers hoped to win the support of all classes of Americans for the cause of independence. When they spoke of "the people" they didn't mean "the mob," as they called them. They did not mean the dirt farmers and tinkers and ship caulkers and sailors and indentured servants and mill workers and slaves and Indians. They meant what they called "the middling people"—the country gentlemen or planters, the merchants and shipowners and lawyers and bankers and yeomen farmers. But needing to unite the greatest number of people to win the Revolution, they didn't talk about the existing inequalities in property, but only about government and political rights. Even today, most of the well-to-do will not publicly admit that where there are gross gaps between rich and poor, people cannot truly have equal rights.

What was meant by the term "created equal"? That in the eyes of nature and of God, every child was *born* equal. Whatever inequalities came to be after birth—those of race, color, sex, class, wealth—could not be blamed upon nature, but on society. That is, on how society operated through government and law. It was social institutions that made blacks and whites unequal, or men and women unequal, or rich and poor unequal, or Christians and Jews unequal. To bring about equality, then, it was up to government to remove barriers and restrictions. The Founding Fathers did not succeed in doing that. (Nor has any government since then, though some have tried, at least to a limited degree.)

This Enlightenment view, that all men are born free and that slavery is contrary to the law of nature, explains how Jefferson the slaveholder could write that "all men are created equal." It was ignorant kings and wicked legislatures that allowed slavery to exist. Enlightened governments would revoke laws that enslaved people. Jefferson would say again and again that in time he expected the American government to abolish slavery and let blacks regain their natural status as free people. Why he failed to free his own slaves will be discussed later.

What about the "pursuit of happiness?" The Enlightenment thinkers believed people were born to be happy. Yet they knew that everywhere people were not happy. Why? Because government, society, religion, prevented it. They stood in the way of our natural yearning for happiness. Here again, however, while the Founding Fathers believed happiness was to be found in freedom, independence, and material comfort, they tended to think it was for whites only.

If being a slave, for instance, prevents happiness, then to eliminate slavery would secure the right to happiness. But slaveholders in Congress did not rush to propose such a move.

So this proclaimed right was a sort of declaration of intent, a hope, an aspiration to those short of rights who needed and demanded them. To others it was only a flourish of fancy words.

Yet, whatever questions are raised about it, the Declaration of Independence was of enormous importance and value worldwide, not only to Jefferson's generation but to all those to come. The ideas in it were not invented by him. But his document was the first to formulate what the world came to see as universally applicable human rights. It was a new thing to state that such rights belong to individuals, and that governments must be constituted to protect the individual's rights against the state itself, as well as against other persons. Which is why the Declaration of Independence still voices what most people in modern societies want and need.

How Jefferson felt about his writing of the Declaration we do not know. He must have written to his wife about it, but after her death he had their correspondence destroyed. We do know that he disliked the "mutilation" of his draft so much that he sent copies of his original to friends, asking them to compare it with the revised version. He got no public acclaim for his achievement during those great days. Nobody asked him to take a bow, and nobody put the spotlight on him. Except for a few friends, no one outside Congress knew he had drafted the Declaration, and no newspaper credited him with it until 1784—eight years later!

At this moment of national jubilation Jefferson was optimistic. He believed it would take the Americans just three months to win the war. He wrote to Virginia begging that a substitute be found to take his seat in Congress. He wanted to go home, he hinted, because his wife was pregnant again, and he meant to be with her during her confinement. It's unclear why Martha's health was so poor. People were much more reserved about such personal matters in those days. Jefferson never explained it even in letters to close friends. Usually Martha wrote to him once a week, and when he missed a mail, he grew frantic. His departure from Philadelphia was delayed, and she probably had a miscarriage in his absence. On September 2, 1776, he resigned his seat in Congress and went home.

For the next three years he would do his best to translate the promise of the Declaration of Independence into a living reality by making Virginia's new government the best it could be.

★ 6 ★

REFORM IN VIRGINIA

Even while working on the Declaration, Jefferson had not been able to get his mind off Virginia. It was in the states, he thought, that the important struggle to form a new government and society would take place. With Virginia voting for independence as he had arrived in Philadelphia in May, he put his mind to work devising a plan for her government. It had to be a better one than the old royal government, or what was the use of revolution?

Sitting in Philadelphia he wrote out three drafts of a detailed plan for a new Virginia constitution and sent the third one south. It arrived in Williamsburg too late, although a few elements of it were inserted into a draft constitution that was almost completed.

Jefferson's draft was in general more democratic than the one adopted. The delegates—moderate men, not radicals—kept many of the old colonial practices that Jefferson angrily called "vicious." No surprise, for the planters meant to keep their political power. It was one thing to lead the break from Britain, but quite another to give up their privileges. Not that Jefferson intended to restructure government in any wildly radical way. He simply wanted somewhat more than the other leaders to realize human rights. Believing that "governments are republican only in proportion as they embody the will of the people and execute it," he favored extending the right to vote. "One half of our brethren who fight and pay taxes," he said, "are excluded . . . from the rights of representation, as if society were instituted for the soil and not for the men inhabiting it." How could the half who had the vote dispose of the rights of the other half, without their consent?

He would not do away with property qualifications, but he wanted to grant suffrage to freeholders owning a quarter of an acre in town or 25 acres in the country. And more: he would grant 50 acres of land to every adult who didn't already have that many. The result would have been the vote for just about every white male. He also urged that representation be based on the number of voters in each district and not on the county unit system, where one county's vote could count more than seventeen times another's. If his point had been taken, it would have lessened the power of the Tidewater rich and added to the power of the growing western region, where he lived.

Although Jefferson believed that the voting privilege was central to living a fully human, democratic life he did not seek to make suffrage truly universal by extending it beyond white males. Twice he argued that women not be given the vote, to "protect" them from the dirty world of politics. As for giving the vote to black Americans, it seems never to have entered his mind.

He was the only Virginia leader to advance his democratic ideas and they were not welcome. Nor were his proposals that the importing of slaves be stopped, and that the official church be disestablished. There was no room for either in a free society, he believed. But the delegates did not listen. They wanted a state controlled by an aristocracy.

Coming back home to Virginia, Jefferson was elected to the House of Burgesses to represent his county. For the next two and a half years he continued his efforts to liberalize the state's social, political, and legal systems. He was happy to be able to spend months at a time with his wife and family at Monticello. Martha still had trouble in childbearing: their only son, born in May 1777, died in a month. But a year later a daughter, Maria, was born who would live into adulthood.

It was in the legislature that Jefferson would initiate the most sweeping movement for reform that any state knew, except perhaps for Pennsylvania. The historian Richard B. Morris paid him tribute by writing, "Of all Americans of that era, Jefferson's commitment to reform proved the most encompassing, and, in terms of his personal commitment, the most enduring."

He served as a legislator from October 1776 until June 1779. Supported by a few other men of stature, he tried to democratize the legal system. In less than three years they proposed 127 bills. Jefferson's first goal was to broaden access to land, to have it distributed more widely so that the power of the landed aristocrats would be lessened. That was one reason why he had tried to have people with less than 50 acres be granted enough to raise their holdings to that size. That having failed, he tried to get the newly elected legislature to pass laws that would bring about substantial redistribution of landholdings. Without going into complex legal details, it is enough to say that though he succeeded in changing some land laws, the net effect was not great. In fact, landownership became more concentrated than ever before in relatively few families. Law gave way to economics and technology.

Not only land law, but Virginia's entire legal code needed revision. A committee of five was elected to do that, with Jefferson chosen to head it. Everyone knew that his understanding of broad principles combined with his meticulous concern for detail would ensure a good outcome.

For the next two and a half years he shouldered most of the work of reforming the laws. The process of introducing bills and getting action dragged on. The legislature took them up not as a whole but one by one. Not until 1785 did the process of consideration end. By that time the war was over and the drive for reform weaker. Only about half the reform bills were adopted.

One of the matters that deeply concerned Jefferson was religious freedom. The notion that religion is a matter of opinion and private choice most Americans take for granted today. But in Jefferson's time that was a revolutionary idea and one that he played a great role in making acceptable.

Although no great crimes like the Inquisition bloodied the pages of colonial history, "persecution for the cause of conscience" was not uncommon. Just before the Revolution, Baptists in Virginia had been thrown into jail for publishing their religious beliefs. Catholic priests were threatened with prison or death. Heresy laws made it a crime to hold certain religious beliefs.

In every colony except Pennsylvania and Rhode Island there was an established church getting economic support from the government. This was plainly special privilege that ran counter to the belief in equality. It was the Congregational Church that enjoyed this privilege in New England; in Virginia and the other colonies it was the Anglican church. Only the established church's clergy could perform marriages, attendance at its service was required, and the whole population was taxed for its support. As Roger Williams once said, and Jefferson believed, "compulsion stinks in God's nostrils." Nor was toleration much better. It was merely a concession from the state, not a right. Handed out as a privilege, it could be taken back. Jefferson believed religion was a private matter, and none of the state's business.

When Virginia had adopted its Declaration of Rights it expressed that principle, but it did not go so far as to disestablish the Anglican Church. As the official church, it was rich and powerful, embracing the cream of society. Although Presbyterians, Lutherans, Baptists, Methodists outnumbered the Anglicans, it didn't matter.

The new Virginia constitution said nothing about this.

Old Bruton Church in Williamsburg, Virginia, the seat of the Anglicans, whose power Jefferson opposed

Members of the dissenting sects pressed the legislature to declare full equality of all religions and to separate the Church from the State. Jefferson was put on a committee to handle the religious issue, together with his younger colleague, James Madison. It began a close friendship that would endure all their lives.

Jefferson's own religious views were deist. That is, he believed in natural religion based on human reasoning rather than revelation. It was better for a country to have many sects rather than one, he thought. Since human happiness depended on freedom of the mind, that must include freedom of religious thought.

He was highly conscious of moral values, taking conscience to be a kind of special moral sense we have, part of our own nature. He found ethical guidance not only in the Scriptures but in the writing of the ancient classical philosophers. But he had little patience with the established Anglican church, opposing its preferred status and special privileges. While most of his friends were Anglicans, he considered the law giving that church special authority oppressive.

His convictions about religious freedom led him into the bitterest and most severe of contests in the Virginia legislature. As a member of the committee on religion he framed a bill on religious freedom early on. But it wasn't introduced until after he was governor. And it was not adopted until 1786, seven years later. His was the strongest voice supporting, in his words, "a wall of separation between Church and State." He said repeatedly that the state had no business supporting or opposing any particular religion or sect. All should be left strictly alone. A true religion does not need the support of law, and no person, either believer or nonbeliever, should be taxed to support a religious institution of any kind. (In time that view found its way into the First Amendment of the Bill of Rights.)

When he learned that his bill was finally enacted in Virginia, shepherded through by James Madison, Jefferson wrote this to him from Paris:

> It is comfortable to see the standard of reason at length erected, after so many ages during which the human mind has been held in vassalage by kings, priests and nobles: and it is honorable for us to have produced the first legislature who had the courage to declare that the reason of man may be trusted with the formation of his own opinions.

Today the Virginia Statute is considered to be one of the most celebrated documents in world history. Nothing that

The young James Madison, whose political skills got Jefferson's Virginia Statute for Religious Freedom adopted by the legislature

Jefferson ever did gave him greater satisfaction. That is why he included it in his epitaph as one of the three great achievements he wished to be remembered for.

Jefferson rewrote all laws dealing with crime and punishment, trying to bring them up to the humane standards of the Enlightenment. Punishment should be proportionate to the injury done, he felt, and the death penalty (horse thieves were executed) limited to murder and treason. Correction and reform were more likely to deter crime than cruel or bloody vengeance. But Jefferson's new criminal code was defeated by a single vote.

Another feature of his reform was a systematic plan for general education. It provided for an elementary education for everyone and university training for superior students. He introduced his plan in late 1778 but it didn't get serious attention until 1786, when James Madison (Jefferson was in Paris) brought it up. Jefferson kept insisting that education was the most important of all reforms needed to secure a vital democracy.

His plan called for three years of free public schooling—very little by today's standards, but in his time Virginia had no public education at all. His was not really a system of equal education for all, but one which sought to develop the most talented children from all classes of society (whites only) in order to create "an aristocracy of virtue and talent." He believed the only way to preserve the republic and prevent those in power from becoming tyrannical was "to illuminate, as far as possible, the minds of the people at large." Those young people "whom nature hath endowed with genius and virtue" should be liberally educated and called to government service regardless of the class they were born into.

Not much of this plan got through the legislature. Only in 1796 was any plan for public schooling adopted. While it used some of Jefferson's inspiring language, it only authorized elementary schools without making them compulsory. It was up to each local community to decide whether it wanted a school. The failure of his plan was disappointing, but Jefferson kept on advancing his ideas for education almost till the day he died.

At the center of Virginia life was slavery. Yet nothing the reform committee did made any change in the laws of slavery. The committee talked of a proposal to emancipate all slaves born after such an act would be passed. An amendment to the law code was prepared that called for gradual emancipation. It provided that children born to slaves should stay with their parents until a certain age, then be trained at public expense in farming or other skills. When the females were eighteen and males twenty-one, they would be colonized outside Virginia "as free and independent" people.

Why outside the state? Because, said Jefferson,

> Deep rooted prejudices entertained by the whites; ten thousand recollections, by the blacks, of the

> injuries they have sustained; new provocations; the real distinctions which nature has made; and many other circumstances, will divide us into parties, and produce convulsions which will probably never end but in the extermination of the one or the other race.

The record does not show that this emancipation measure was ever introduced. Jefferson said much later it was because "the public mind would not yet bear the proposition." Slavery was far too solidly rooted to be abolished by the idealism nourished by the Revolution. So Jefferson decided to bide his time, waiting for public opinion to change.

The law reform is another example of what little recognition Jefferson got for a great achievement. When the legislature chose not to adopt the committee report as a whole, but take it up item by item, it blurred the public's perception of what had been done. Only those few aware of the years of unstinting intellectual labor knew what Jefferson's contribution had been. Madison said later that the law code was perhaps the hardest public task Jefferson had undertaken in his entire career. And even though not all of it had been accepted, it proved to be "a mine of legislative wealth" and a model of fine lawmaking.

7

A GOVERNOR IN WARTIME

Just after he turned thirty-six, Jefferson began to talk about retiring from public life. His friends reproved him. You are too young to drop out of politics, they said. You have too much to offer the rising generation. There's still much to be done. They nominated him for governor, and he reluctantly went along. The election was not by popular vote, but by the Virginia assembly. He won, and it opened up one of the most miserable chapters of his life.

He took office in June 1779. The Revolutionary War was in its fourth year. There was no time to use his office for social reform. The British forces had opened up a new front in the southern states. To be governor in wartime imposed responsibilities no one would welcome. To make it worse, his office had small authority and few of the resources needed to meet the military crisis. The legislature held supreme power; he could do little without its consent.

Soon after his election the delegates voted that the state capital be moved from Williamsburg to Richmond, a more central location and one less vulnerable to the invading Brit-

The Governor's Palace at Williamsburg, where Jefferson resided as second governor of Virginia. The capital was later moved to Richmond.

ish. Jefferson rented a brick house in Richmond, only a hamlet then, and brought in forty-eight crates of household furnishings from the governor's palace at Williamsburg that he had so briefly occupied. No sooner was he in residence than he began to draw up plans for making the town a handsome state capital. But the war was moving so close to him that he had to concentrate on military needs. What to do about enlisting more troops, gathering arms, clothing, supplies?

In that spring of 1780 the Americans were in terrible trouble. The Treasury was empty, the public credit exhausted, the army draining away, the people and Congress quarreling. General Washington pleaded with Jefferson to get clothing for the Virginia troops sent to fight in South Carolina. But in May Charleston was taken by the British and 5,000 Americans surrendered, including the Virginians. Just as he heard the disastrous news, Jefferson was reelected to a second term as governor.

As the British army moved north from Charleston toward Virginia, Jefferson's situation became even more desperate. The state was broke, inflation making its currency worthless. Jefferson could furnish no supplies to his own militia. The soldiers he sent south to meet the British advance in North Carolina came without arms or ammunition or even adequate clothing.

Whose fault was it? Plainly the state had failed years before to mobilize properly for a war that would drag on so long. The legislature had not done its job, and Jefferson, as one of its members, shared in the blame. He did all he could now, plunging into the crucial problems of supply and distribution, worrying over every detail, writing letters and orders to speed action, and sending reports to General Washington and the Congress on the military situation in his region.

He could not count on the full support of his own Virginians. From the onset of the Revolution it was clear that about a third of the American colonists were Patriots, another third were Tories, or Loyalists, siding with the British, and the last third, neutral. There were enough Loyalists to endanger the Revolution, and they were especially numerous in the south. Virginia had its sizable share of them, and they made Jefferson's task so much harder. One army leader exploded in fury when he saw so many Virginians standing around idle while he suffered for lack of troops.

With manpower so short, not only in Virginia but throughout the country, some prominent officers, such as Colonel Alexander Hamilton and Colonel John Laurens, began to call for enlistment of blacks, both slave and free. General Nathaniel Greene reported that the black volunteers he had seen in action were "formidable" fighters. What was Jefferson's response to the proposal? According to the historian John C. Miller, this was his thinking:

> Jefferson . . . did not welcome blacks as soldiers. While admitting that they sometimes displayed courage, he attributed their value to their inability fully to appreciate the peril in which their actions placed them. Nor did he believe that they were conditioned by slavery to make good soldiers: they were too conscious of the degradation they had suffered at the hands of whites, he said, to fight zealously for the freedom of their masters. Finally, he stood in far too much dread of slave insurrections to approve of the idea of putting guns—together with the intoxicating slogans promising liberty and equality to all men—in the hands of blacks. Instead of regarding the black population as a potential reservoir of fighting men, Jefferson, throughout the war, acted on the assumption that neither free blacks nor free slaves could be safely trusted with arms.

So even though not nearly enough white Virginians joined the armed forces, Jefferson exerted no leadership in recruiting blacks to help in the crisis. The legislature refused to permit slaves to enlist in the Continental Army or the state militia; instead it offered 300 acres, or one young and healthy Negro, or a sum of money to any white males who would enlist.

Jefferson's ideas about individual liberty were so paramount that it weakened his ability to get things done in wartime. Because people disliked being drafted, he hesitated to call out the militia and then hastened to dismiss them. When men were needed to build fortifications he said you can't get freemen to do work fit only for slaves. Even slaveholders, he said, could not be ordered to lend their slaves for military labor. Only at the last, when the British commander Lord Cornwallis faced the American troops at Yorktown, did he ask the legislature to permit him to draft slaves to work as laborers with the state militia. In the end, Virginia used more slave labor to win the war than any other state.

War service, however, brought only a few slaves their freedom. But not their citizenship, for Virginia declared only free white persons could be citizens.

The war came to Jefferson's doorstep in January 1781. A British fleet sailed up the James River and landed an army to attack Richmond. Jefferson moved government records and supplies out of the town and sent his family away to safety. The British entered Richmond, destroyed a foundry, burned some buildings, and carried off whatever arms and equipment were still there. Then they left, and the government returned. Late in May the British again invaded Richmond, but the legislators had escaped to meet in Charlottesville. Jefferson, on his way there, stopped at Monticello. With his second term as governor ending on June 2, he had decided not to seek a third one-year term. This might have seemed like desertion in the face of the enemy, but he reasoned that the man sure to replace him was General Thomas Nelson, commander of the state militia. And to concentrate military and civil power in one man's hands at this point would be best. He himself, he said, was not a man educated to command armies.

Meanwhile the British sent 250 cavalrymen to raid Charlottesville in the hope of capturing the legislature and the governor. Luckily a military scout spotted the cavalry beginning its move and rode all night to warn Jefferson and the legislature. They fled, Jefferson escaping on horseback through the woods just as the cavalry began to ride up to Monticello.

The British entered Charlottesville on June 4. Jefferson's term as governor had ended two days before, but the harried legislature, meeting this time in Staunton, had not had time to elect his successor. Jefferson was not there; he had taken his family to his farm in Poplar Forest, 90 miles from Monticello. Since everyone knew his term had ended and he would not accept another, he saw no reason why he should be in Staunton. For eight days, until June 12, when Nelson was chosen governor, the state was without a chief executive. Jefferson's absence in time of crisis brought "volumes of reproach" upon him, "serious or sarcastic," as he said. He was accused of cowardice, and of being inept in military matters. The day the legislature convened, the members voted that at its first session inquiry should be made into the conduct of the governor during the past twelve months.

At that session, Jefferson stood up and answered one by one the rumors spread about him. When he finished, the legislators passed unanimously a resolution of commendation and thanks for his service. He had been publicly cleared of any wrongdoing but he felt bitter that his honor had been attacked unfairly, and only on the basis of rumor.

Now he was even more determined to keep his pledge to withdraw from public life. The Continental Congress that June asked him to become one of the five commissioners to go to Paris to negotiate a peace with Great Britain. He refused, writing that "I have taken my final leave of everything of that nature, have retired to my farm, my family and books, from which I think nothing will ever separate me."

The Surrender of Lord Cornwallis at Yorktown,
painted by John Trumbull

A few months later the war was over. With the powerful help of a French fleet and French troops, Washington had trapped the British at Yorktown. On October 19, 1781, with his food and supplies melting away, and under steady bombardment from French and American guns, Lord Cornwallis was forced to give up. He surrendered his entire army of 7,000 men. There was sporadic fighting for a year more, but in reality the revolution had been won.

Besides the damage done to his reputation while governor, Jefferson suffered heavy personal losses from the war.

On one of their raids into Virginia, the British had made one of Jefferson's estates their headquarters. They moved out in ten days, leaving behind burned tobacco barns, wasted crops, slaughtered animals. They carried off thirty of Jefferson's slaves, twenty-seven of whom died of fever or disease. He didn't know what happened to the other three. In addition, twenty-two of Jefferson's own slaves were among the thousands of Virginia slaves who fled to the British side.

In the spring of 1782 a French nobleman, Chastellux, a major general in the French army sent to help the Americans, paid a visit to Monticello. He reported that his host was a charming man, describing him as ". . . not yet forty, tall, and with a mild and pleasing countenance, but whose mind and attainments could serve in lieu of all outward graces; an American, who, without ever having quitted his own country, is Musician, Draftsman, Surveyor, Astronomer, Natural Philosopher, Jurist, and Statesman . . . and finally a Philosopher." He mentioned too Jefferson's "gentle and amiable wife," and their "charming children whose education is his special care."

The guest had come at a happy time, the war over and public cares ended, but it was not to last long. In May another daughter was born—the second to be named Lucy Elizabeth, for the first had died in infancy only a year earlier. But there was no time to rejoice: Mrs. Jefferson emerged from childbirth dangerously ill. She never recovered. Jefferson was helpless. For four months, constantly at her bedside to nurse her, he watched her life slip away. On September 6, 1782, in his account book Jefferson wrote, "My dear wife died this day at 11:45 a.m." Much as he hungered for affection, Jefferson never married again.

A moment before his wife died, his daughter Martha recalled later, "he was led from the room in a state of insensibility by his sister, Mrs. Carr, who, with great difficulty, got him into the library where he fainted, and remained so long insensible that they feared he never would revive." After the burial he went to his room and stayed there for three weeks, pacing up and down, day and night, sleeping only when completely exhausted. When he went out at last, it was to ride his horse over the mountains and through the woods, sunk in melancholy.

It took five weeks for him to emerge from that deadness of mind and spirit, though friends and family did their best to comfort him. He was surrounded by a much-enlarged family. Shortly before his wife's death Jefferson had welcomed his sister Martha, widow of Dabney Carr, and her six children into his household. Now there were nine children at Monticello, the eldest of whom, Peter Carr, he treated like a beloved son. To all of them he would give much time and care.

To get him away from the scene of sorrow, the Congress again offered to send him to France, to help the commission completing the negotiations for peace. He accepted at once, but before he could sail a provisional peace treaty was signed.

He welcomed the news of success but regretted missing a trip to France. However, he had taken the first step back toward public life, and was ready to serve again. In June 1783 the chance came when the Virginians elected him to Congress.

★ 8 ★

CONGRESSMAN WITH IDEAS

The last act in Jefferson's career as a lawmaker was his service in the Continental Congress. It came at the end of the American Revolution and would last for only six months. Remember that this Congress functioned under the Articles of Confederation. That shaky form of government, sketched out in 1776, had not been ratified by the states until 1781. It rapidly proved too weak and inadequate. The states all through the war quarreled among themselves over boundaries, over tariffs, over court decisions. The members had to flee from Philadelphia whenever threatened by British actions, and bad weather and poor transportation often interfered with attendance. So did the plain irresponsibility of many delegates. It might take months to get a quorum together—nine states were required for major decisions, and often not more than six states showed up. Nor did the quality of the delegates impress Jefferson. Many thought their private affairs more important than the nation's.

When Jefferson was elected to Congress he decided to take his daughter Martha and to place her with good friends in Philadelphia, where she would be with other children. With Mrs. Jefferson sick for so long, she had not had much mothering, and Jefferson tried his best to make up for it. He planned a heavy course of reading for her; it would have made her one of the best-educated women in America. He secured tutors in French, painting, and dancing. Now he began to write his children, telling them of some interesting event while always prescribing what to do to improve their personal appearance, conduct, and work habits. But he forgot how young the girls were. (They never wrote as frequently as he did.) The tone of his letters could be intimidating. In his first one to Martha, for instance, he schedules her studies from 8 A.M. to bedtime and adds, "The acquirements which I hope you will make under the tutors I have provided for you will render you more worthy of my love, and if they cannot increase it they will prevent its diminution." And he concluded: "If you love me then, strive to be good under every situation and to all living creatures, and to acquire those accomplishments which I have put in your power, and which will go far towards ensuring you the warmest love of your affectionate father."

With Martha settled in, Jefferson went on to Annapolis, where the Congress was to meet. Forced to wait two weeks before enough members appeared to conduct business, he carried on his weather observations and browsed for works of science in the bookstores. When the Congress at last got down to work, he was made chairman of several committees. The most important had the task of deciding how the West should be opened up to settlement.

It should be noted that the charters of six states (the Carolinas, Connecticut, Georgia, Massachusetts, and Virginia) had set the Pacific Ocean as a western boundary. It was expected that beyond the settled regions, the lands would be conquered by the Continental Army. The smaller states feared that unless the United States took over the western region, the states that claimed them would have a huge economic and political advantage. They wanted all states to be on an equal footing, with the western lands given to the nation.

The building at Annapolis, Maryland, where the Continental Congress met in 1783. Jefferson headed the committee on the western regions.

Jefferson's own state had just given up its claim to territory north and west of the Ohio River and made the Congress custodian of millions of acres of arable land. Once the Indians were removed, sales of acreage to settlers could help meet the financial needs of the Congress and add new states to the Union.

Jefferson's committee developed a plan for the temporary government of the western territory. It was called the Ordinance of 1784. The opening of the West provided a great opportunity to create a society of self-sufficient farmers, the kind of people Jefferson regarded as the backbone of the democracy. Unless the Congress took quick action, however, speculators and monopolizers would surely grab the land. So the Ordinance placed landownership within the reach of most citizens.

Jefferson knew he could influence the course of American history through the Ordinance. He felt that to separate from the British Empire only to found an American empire with future Westerners as second-class citizens would be tragically wrong. He believed that the growing Union should provide against making the new region subordinate to the old. Nor should the old states be swamped by the new. He wanted a Union of equals among all the states. He therefore proposed that new states of roughly equal size be formed from the Western lands and that each be admitted to the Union on an equal basis with the original thirteen states.

The most striking aspect of the plan for the 1784 Ordinance had to do with slavery. To interest yeomen farmers in settling out West, Jefferson and others felt the region should be closed to slavery. Yeomen farmers would not want to compete with a plantation system relying upon slave labor. (He had observed that himself in Virginia.) So in the committee's draft of the Ordinance, a ban on slavery was applied to all the territories of the Union, south as well as north of the Ohio, after 1800.

Was this something the Articles of Confederation permitted? No: Jefferson knew that slavery was considered a matter of state concern, and that the Articles gave Congress no power to prohibit slavery in the territories. Yet he stood for a broad interpretation of the inherent power of Congress to legislate for goals it believed essential to the national welfare.

However, Congress rejected the clause banning slavery—by a margin of just one vote. "Thus," wrote Jefferson much later, "we see the fate of millions unborn hanging on the tongue of one man, and heaven was silent in that awful moment." That one vote, which would have been in favor of the ban, was lost when a New Jersey delegate fell sick and couldn't come in to cast his ballot.

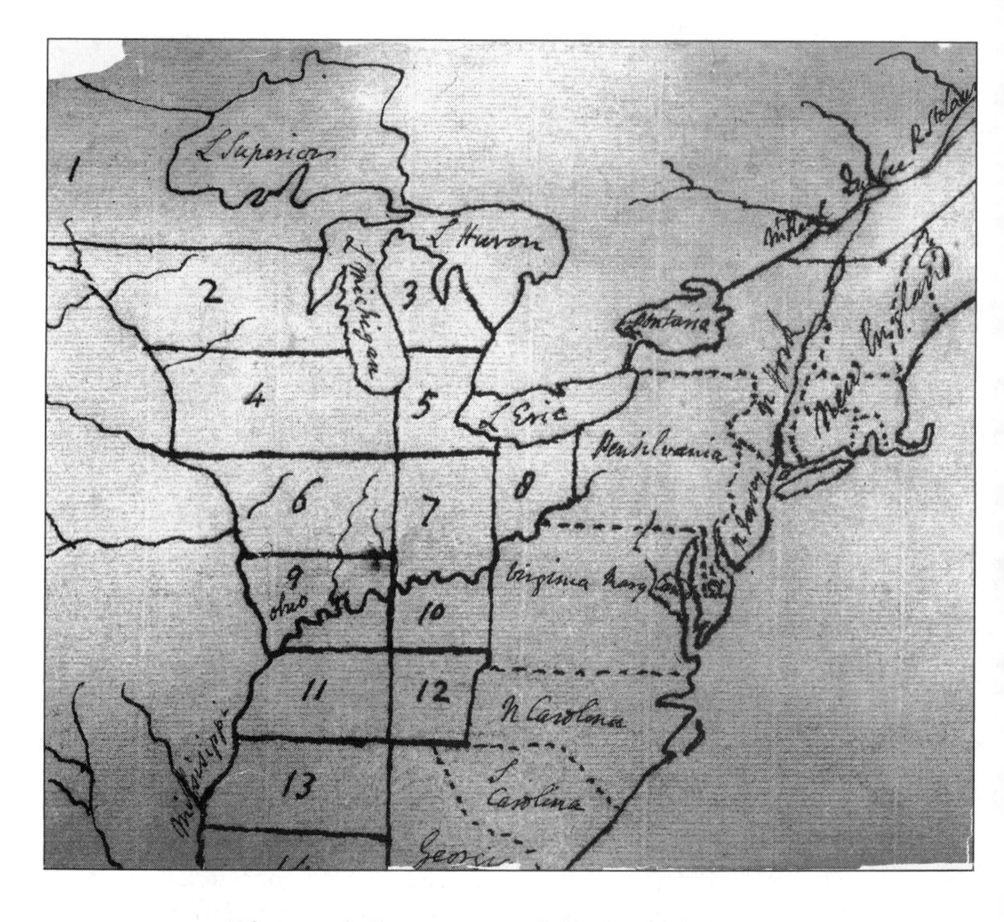

The map Jefferson prepared for the Ordinance of 1784 shows the roughly equal-sized states he wanted to be formed out of the western lands.

Soon the Ordinance of 1787 replaced that of 1784, retaining the essentials of the earlier one. In the 1787 measure, however, slavery was prohibited, though only in the region northwest of the Ohio River. Other provisions of the Ordinance guaranteed to Westerners civil rights and liberties, religious freedom, and education. All future territorial acquisitions would be regulated in this pattern.

The coinage of the country was a mess, and Jefferson made proposals to bring order out of chaos. The various gold and silver coins used in the states had different values, complicating the doing of business. Jefferson proposed basing a new system on the Spanish silver dollar, widely used. He insisted the dollar be subdivided on the basis of tenths and hundredths. "The bulk of mankind are schoolboys throughout life," he said, and money arithmetic should be made as simple as possible. He wanted to drop the British pounds, shillings, pence, and farthings, replacing it with the decimal system. Congress liked his proposal and took it over. It is the system we use today.

Jefferson's role in the Congress again typified his dislike of public controversy. He called the debates "very contentious," and would have no part in the angry exchanges of delegates who couldn't listen to any argument that was not their own. In his many years as a legislator he had found that in public assemblies people fought so bitterly that it wrecked private friendships. But how could it be otherwise, he wondered, in assemblies made up mostly of lawyers, "whose trade it is to question everything, yield nothing and talk by the hour?"

When the Revolutionary War ended, Congress began to think about how best to work out friendly relations with the European powers and how to conduct business with their people. The obvious course was to negotiate treaties to this effect. America already had three ministers in Europe: John Adams, Benjamin Franklin, and John Jay—all northerners—and the southern states demanded that another minister be added to represent their commercial interests. Jefferson some months earlier had prepared instructions for the ministers, and since he knew what was wanted, Congress elected the Virginian to go abroad and share in the treaty negotiations.

★ 9 ★

PARIS—AND NOTES ON SLAVERY

Like most visitors then and now, Jefferson came to Paris with romantic expectations. At first he found "the city of light" disappointing. The streets were narrow, crowded, unpaved, and frequent rain could leave them deep in mud. The noise, the bustle were unrelenting. The water was unhealthy, the air damp.

That first winter he was sick much of the time. The gloom turned to despair when news came from home that a whooping cough epidemic had taken away his youngest child, Lucy Elizabeth, two and a half. Maria, his six-year-old, had managed to overcome the disease. Left with only two children, he determined to have Maria join him and Martha in Paris. All sorts of complications delayed it; only two years later did she arrive.

He moved twice before he found the house he liked. It was an elegant mansion bordering the Champs-Elysées, with large grounds and a garden, where he grew Indian corn for his table. The rent was too much, but he never stinted on himself. He would pile expenses high by remodeling places he lived in only temporarily and buying more and better furniture than he needed. He hired a staff of servants and kept a carriage and two horses. He wore knee breeches, lace ruffles, silk stockings, and an embroidered waistcoat, and powdered hair. Fashion in Paris was dictatorial, and he followed along. Raised as an aristocrat he took luxury for granted. Besides, an American minister abroad had to maintain his country's dignity. So everything had to be of the best. Sometimes at dinner this generous host had as many as eighteen guests. The salary the young republic paid its diplomats—and rarely on time!—was far below what he spent, and he went deeply into debt.

Martha must go on with her education. Jefferson decided on a convent school rated the most genteel in Paris and got her admitted on the recommendation of a French nobleman. The nuns taught about sixty girls, three of them princesses. Martha wore the crimson uniform, was nicknamed "Jeffy," and soon was getting along happily in French. Her father visited her often and, when official duties kept him away, wrote to her. He was relieved to find that the students included as many Protestants as Catholics, and that the nuns spoke not a word about religion.

As his first year in France was ending, Jefferson wrote friends how he felt about the country. "I find the general fate of humanity here the most deplorable. . . ." Nineteen of the twenty million people, he was convinced, were "more wretched, more accursed in every circumstance of human existence, than the most conspicuously wretched individual of the whole United States." The workers, the peasants, the poor suffered terribly under the oppression of the upper classes. As for the privileged ones, the younger thought only about their love affairs while the older thought only about ambition. What he did value was the polished manners, the courtesy shown by French society. No one was rude to another; no one drank to excess. It was French culture he prized above all—its music, painting, sculpture, architecture.

As soon as he had arrived in Paris, Jefferson had called on Dr. Benjamin Franklin, the elder statesman on duty here since 1776. Suffering from painful illness, Franklin kept to his house in Passy, where the much younger Jefferson visited him often. John Adams, the other member of the negotiating team, was living in Auteuil with his wife, Abigail, and two of their grown children. Closer in age, John and Abigail welcomed him frequently to their home.

Two young men had recently arrived to become part of Jefferson's staff and household. Colonel David Humphrey, a recent aide of George Washington's, was in Paris as secretary of the American commission, and William Short, a Virginian protégé of Jefferson's, had come to serve as his private secretary.

Negotiating for commercial treaties with the European nations proved a nearly hopeless task. Why were the best efforts of the commission so fruitless? Because America was a new nation, weak from her long war for independence, small in population, inexperienced in diplomacy. The glowing response of many Europeans to her fight for freedom was fading. Her desire to break into the closed economic systems of the maritime powers was treated with indifference, if not disdain. What America asked for was not acceptable to them. They had little confidence in the future of the shaky new republic. They felt they did not need America; nor had they anything to fear from her.

After breaking free of British domination of her commerce, America hoped to wiggle through the trade barriers of other nations. So she appealed for freedom of trade, proposing commercial agreements that would be of mutual benefit. America had major surplus products she wanted to sell abroad—rice, tobacco, fish, lumber, furs. And she had the ships to carry the trade, whether to Europe or the European colonies in the West Indies. But even if a hint of progress was in the wind, it was wiped out when the other side would ask, how do we know if the individual American states will respect any agreement made by the Congress? Europe was well aware of what little power the Articles of Confederation left to the Congress.

Franklin, now seventy-nine, went home early in 1785, with Jefferson elected by the Congress to replace him as minister to France. And Adams left for London, to become minister to England. For the next four years Jefferson would conduct diplomacy on his own. It was a critical time to be away from home, where a new constitution would be drafted, followed by a close contest for its ratification and then a struggle for the adoption of a Bill of Rights.

Negotiating treaties was one part of Jefferson's duty; making friends with the French was another. When the press spread bad rumors about America it was his job to try to correct them. Now that the period of generous aid to the American cause was over, the monarchy paid little attention to affairs across the sea. Jefferson tried to keep the court informed of his country's needs and interests. He assured all foreigners he met that America was in good shape and in no danger of collapse. In this he had the help of the Marquis de Lafayette and other French officers who had also served under Washington. In command of an American division in the Yorktown campaign, Lafayette, then only twenty-four, had earned great honor. The two men had become warm friends while Jefferson was Virginia's governor. Even before Jefferson left for France, Lafayette had talked with him about founding a colony of free blacks in western Virginia to demonstrate that former slaves could do as well under freedom as whites.

More important than newspapers in shaping French opinion were books. Here Jefferson's desire "to promote the general good of mankind by an interchange of useful things" had its best opportunity. Whatever was published in America that reflected her concern for political and intellectual freedom he brought to the attention of the French. The finest contribution to Europe's knowledge of America was a work from his own hand, his *Notes on the State of Virginia.* This was a book, the only book he would ever write. It was first printed in France (not in America) some nine months after he arrived. But most of it had been written four years earlier, in the months after his governorship of Virginia ended.

This is how the book came about. In September 1780 a Monsieur Marbois, secretary to the French minister to America, sent state governors and other prominent Americans a list of twenty-two questions. He hoped their answers would give him and his government information about the new nation that might be helpful.

But only two people replied: Jefferson and General John Sullivan, who made a rather casual response. Jefferson, on the other hand, took the trouble to prepare over 300 pages in reply. Marbois wanted to know about *everything*—population, natural resources, geography, geology, the Indians, government, law, the economy, education, religion, the military, history. Analysis was not what he asked for; rather it was plain facts, the mass of information the French intellectuals of that time loved to collect and assemble in huge dictionaries or encyclopedias.

The request came as Jefferson's final term in the governor's office was ending. He had returned to Monticello and, while out riding, had fallen from his horse. His injuries kept him at home, and never one to waste a moment he took up Marbois's inquiries. It excited him; this "mysterious obligation" would make him much better informed about his own country than he had ever been before, he said. Not quite true, for no one knew more about Virginia than Jefferson. He had built up over the years unmatched private archives of material on his beloved state and country. He kept careful records of everything his insatiable curiosity steered him to, wanting the data to be useful not just to himself but to others. The book that came out of this work is a factual guide to America. It is also a defense against slanders Europeans had hurled against her, and his interpretation of what the

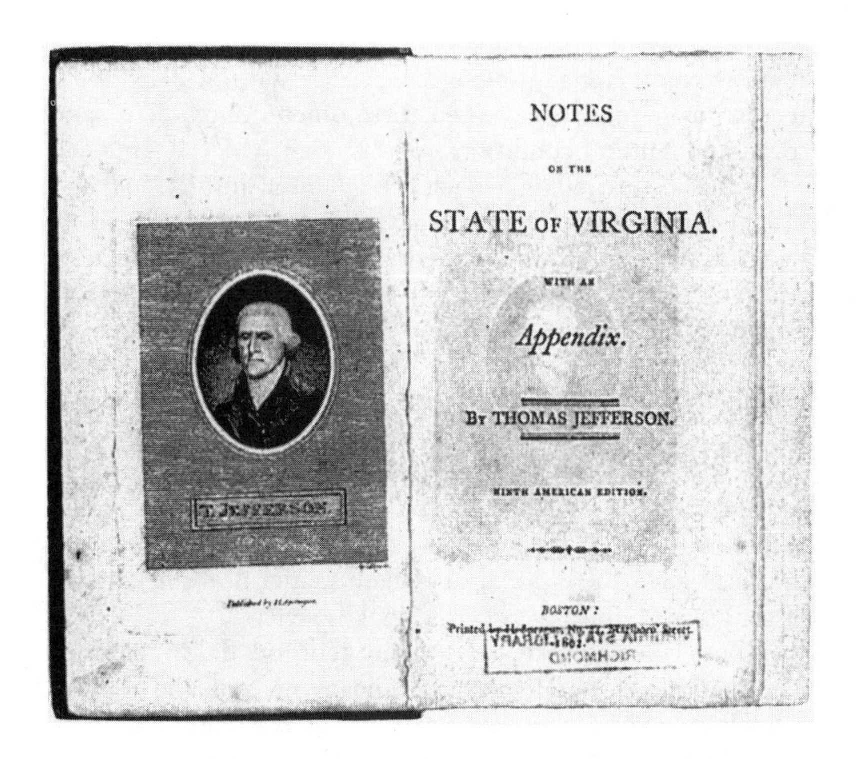

T. JEFFERSON.

NOTES

ON THE

STATE OF VIRGINIA.

WITH AN

Appendix.

BY THOMAS JEFFERSON.

NINTH AMERICAN EDITION.

BOSTON:

The title page and frontispiece of the 1802 edition of Jefferson's Notes on the State of Virginia

American Enlightenment stood for. In essence it represents his social philosophy. Today the book is seen as one of the most important scientific and political works to come out of eighteenth-century America.

In December 1781 Jefferson finished a draft and sent it to Marbois. But he wasn't satisfied and began to revise his answers. Over the next few years he improved and enlarged the work before allowing it to be printed in 1785.

On some topics raised by Marbois he had much more to say than on others. Although he centered on Virginia, he moved beyond it on some subjects, such as the Native Americans, to whom he gave a whole chapter, arguing that they were probably equal in mind and body to any European. That there were differences among peoples he did not deny. But it was not nature that created these differences. No, it was social and cultural conditions.

The longest chapter dealt with natural history and included detailed lists of trees, plants, animals, and birds. In it he tried to prove wrong the theory of Buffon, a noted French naturalist, who claimed that the animals and aborigines of America were smaller than and inferior to their European counterparts. Jefferson bolstered his case with data gathered from many people who measured and weighed animals at his request. He was countering the arguments of many Europeans that nature itself had doomed America to degeneracy.

He used the *Notes* to refute the charge of another Frenchman, Abbé Raynal, who said, "America has not yet produced a good poet, a capable mathematician, a single man of genius in a single art or in a single science."

But, Jefferson asked, how many centuries did it take the Greeks to produce a Homer, the Romans a Vergil, the French a Racine and Voltaire, the English a Shakespeare and Milton? When the United States has existed as long without producing a genius, then it will be time for reproach. But he went on to cite Franklin in physics, Rittenhouse in astronomy, Washington in war, than whom no one in Europe had shown greater genius in their fields. Yet we have only three million inhabitants, while Britain has ten million and France, twenty million. With those ratios they should have produced many more such eminent men. Where were they?

Another long section of the book describes the constitution and laws of Virginia. Here he was sharply critical of the denial of the vote to a large number of freemen as well as the concentration of power—legislative, executive, and judicial—in a single branch of government, the legislature. Even such a group of men, their power unchecked, could produce a tyranny.

Coming to manufactures, Jefferson wrote a much quoted passage that sets farming far above manufacturing in his scale of values:

> Those who labor in the earth are the chosen people of God, if ever He had a chosen people, whose breasts He has made his peculiar deposit for substantial and genuine virtue. . . . While we have land to labor then, let us never wish to see our citizens occupied at a workbench, or twirling a distaff. Carpenters, masons, smiths, are wanting in husbandry: but, for the general operations of manufacture, let our workshops remain in Europe. . . . The mobs of great cities add just so much to the support of pure government, as sores do to the strength of the human body. . . .

To him agriculture was more than farming; it was a way of life. He gave much of his life to public service, but he always thought of himself as a farmer. At the time he wrote the *Notes* he owned thirteen farms.

When he wrote that "those who labor in the earth are the chosen people of God," he was thinking only of whites. As one man remarked unkindly, if that were true, the blacks must be the chosen people in Virginia for they did most of that kind of labor. On Jefferson's own plantations it was cheap slave labor that made his luxurious style of living possible. He may have thought of himself as a humane slave master, but he was the beneficiary of a system which was the negation of humanity.

Marbois had not asked about slavery in America. (Perhaps he was embarrassed to raise the question.) But Jefferson brought it up himself. And what he said about it reflects how keenly he saw into the tragic subject and how troubled he was by it:

> There must doubtless be an unhappy influence on the manners of our people produced by the existence of slavery among us. The whole commerce between master and slave is a perpetual exercise of the most boisterous passions, the most

Slave labor under
the eye of a plantation overseer,
as sketched by Benjamin Latrobe

unremitting despotism on the one part, and degrading submissions on the other. Our children see this and learn to imitate it. . . . The parent storms, the child looks on, catches the lineaments of wrath, puts on the same airs in the circle of smaller slaves, gives a loose to the worst of passions, and thus nursed, educated, and daily exercised in tyranny, cannot but be stamped by it with odious peculiarities. The man must be a prodigy who can retain his manners and morals undepraved by such circumstances. And with what execration should the statesman be loaded who, permitting one half the citizens to trample on the rights of the other,

> transforms those into despots, and these into enemies, destroys the morals of the one part and the amor patriae of the other. . . . With the morals of the people, their industry is also destroyed. For in a warm climate no man will labor for himself who can make another labor for him. . . .
>
> And can the liberties of a nation be thought secure when we have removed their only firm basis, a conviction in the minds of the people that these liberties are of the gift of God? That they are not to be violated but with His wrath? Indeed I tremble for my country when I reflect that God is just; that his justice cannot sleep forever; that considering numbers, nature and natural means only, a revolution of the wheel of fortune, an exchange of situation, is among possible events; that it may become probable by supernatural interference. The Almighty has no attribute which can take side with us in such a contest.

We have already seen what he had tried to do about slavery. Back in 1770, arguing in court for the freedom of a third-generation mulatto, he had pleaded that "we are all born free" and that slavery was contrary to nature, a plea the court rejected. In 1776, drafting the Declaration, he had tried to link the political rights of Americans with the personal rights of slaves, but the Continental Congress had blotted out that passage. A few months later in the Virginia Assembly he had brought in a bill to end the importation of slaves. (Two years later Virginia enacted that ban.) In the same year, working on the revision of Virginia's laws, he had proposed the emancipation of all slaves born after 1800, with the freed people to be educated and colonized at public expense. Rejected. And in 1785 he had tried, and failed, to introduce a clause into the Western Ordinance barring slavery from the territory after 1800.

He was well aware of how ambiguous were the thinking and behavior of men like himself. He put it this way in a letter to a Frenchman:

> What a stupendous, what an incomprehensible, machine is man, who can endure toil, famine, stripes, imprisonment and death itself in vindication of his own liberty, and the next moment be deaf to all those motives whose power supported him through his trial, and inflict on his fellow-men a bondage, one hour of which is fraught with more misery than ages of that which he rose in rebellion to oppose.

As much as his Virginia was based on slavery, so was it based on race prejudice. From the beginning, the African slave trade and racism had gone together. Which came first it would be useless to debate. In all times and in all places people have tended to treat "outsiders" or "strangers" with contempt, fear, and even hatred. From the days of Columbus the Europeans who came to the New World despised and enslaved the people they outnumbered. Masters always see their victims as inferior to themselves, and fit only for servitude. And then, quite conveniently, they turn this upside down and say, because these people are slaves, they are inferior.

What were Jefferson's own views on this issue? He tried to apply the scientific methods of his time to the study of African-Americans. He asked, to what extent were the differences between black and white Americans due to environment, and to what extent due to biological, that is, inborn factors? Of course he knew that most of the blacks he observed were slaves whereas the whites were free. And he was aware of what great differences in opportunity and education this made for. In the *Notes* he offered a list of abilities or talents in which he judged blacks to be superior, equal, or inferior to whites. Admitting that more research was needed,

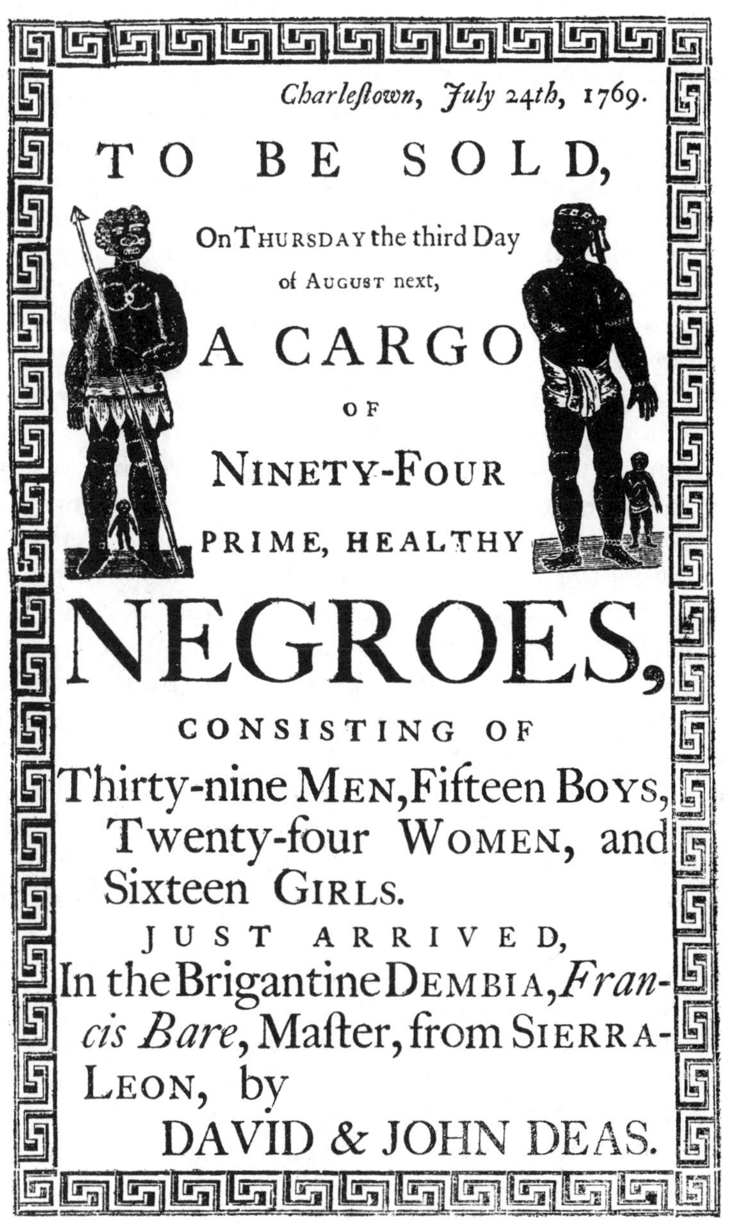

Charlestown, July 24th, 1769.

TO BE SOLD,

On THURSDAY the third Day of AUGUST next,

A CARGO OF NINETY-FOUR PRIME, HEALTHY

NEGROES,

CONSISTING OF

Thirty-nine MEN, Fifteen BOYS, Twenty-four WOMEN, and Sixteen GIRLS.

JUST ARRIVED,

In the Brigantine DEMBIA, *Francis Bare*, Master, from SIERRA-LEON, by

DAVID & JOHN DEAS.

A broadside of 1769, advertising the auction of ninety-four Africans just arrived on a slave ship

he proposed tentatively that African-Americans were superior to whites in music and equal to them in courage, memory, adventurousness, and moral sense. But they were inferior to whites in reasoning power, forethought, poetry, and imagination. He admitted that slavery had robbed the black of "all." Still, he argued that Nature had created a hierarchy among the various races. And the elements of inferiority in blacks that he pointed to he believed had nothing to do with their enslavement. Blacks, he said, in all probability were incapable of great achievement in the higher reaches of the intellect, such as mathematics, science, and literature.

When he suggested that blacks were inferior to whites in some respects, Jefferson stood in opposition to the basic thought of the Enlightenment: that all humankind was essentially the same, and the diversity to be found among peoples was the result of environmental circumstances. Jefferson even went so far as to suggest that blacks might be a separate creation, assigned a different order in the scale of being. His old mentor, George Mason, condemned that theory as false and pernicious. And another good friend, Dr. Benjamin Rush, disagreed too, comparing the various peoples of the earth to one immense extended family.

Though he called his views on race only "suspicions," subject to change on more evidence, in private letters and conversation he was far more dogmatic. He said to a British diplomat, in 1807, that he considered blacks "to be as inferior to the rest of mankind as the mule is to the horse, and as made to carry burdens."

Benjamin Banneker, a free black tobacco planter of Maryland, tried to convince Jefferson that whites and blacks were equal in intellectual capacity. A self-taught mathematician and astronomer, Banneker sent Jefferson the manuscript of an astronomical study he had prepared, as proof that all men are created equal, with qualities and capacities un-

A woodcut of Benjamin Banneker, taken from his almanac of 1795

related to race. He hoped Jefferson would welcome proof of this, while implying that Jefferson was violating his own principles in holding black people in slavery.

Jefferson replied courteously, and got Banneker appointed surveyor in the District of Columbia, where the new federal capital was to be built. But he sent Banneker's study to a French friend, asserting that one black mathematician did not prove that black people were equal to whites in intellectual powers. Later he even called Banneker's letters to him "very childish and trivial." To the end Jefferson continued to be skeptical or dismissive of black intellectual achievement. Whenever he heard of a distinguished black he would habitually ask how much "white blood" that person possessed.

When he wrote of black inferiority, Jefferson cut the ground from under his appeal for emancipation. The slave masters regarded the alleged inferiority as an undeniable fact, and to them that justified slavery as the proper condition for all nonwhites. It was the plan of the Almighty that blacks should be created inferior in order to serve whites.

That dogma of racial inferiority took deep root in American scholarship. Most anthropologists, sociologists, and historians, as late as the 1920s, took it as an unassailable scientific truth. Jefferson's words, coupled with his immense prestige, would do great damage to the cause of emancipation and civil rights. He set the tone for the racial prejudice that continues to sap the American faith in the natural and inalienable rights of a free and equal people.

When you think about it you realize how powerful was the psychological pressure on Jefferson to believe that blacks were innately inferior. How could he live with himself if he thought that he and his fellow Virginians held down in slavery untold numbers of potential scientists, poets, philosophers, statesmen, artists? By clinging to his "suspicions" of the inferiority of blacks, he preserved some sort of inner balance (tormented at times), always consoling himself with the belief that slavery was only temporary; it would die someday, somehow.

When Jefferson answered the queries of Marbois he did not intend for his views to be made public. His words were only for the French to consider. So he freely voiced his dislike for that "hideous evil," slavery. He knew Virginians would not like to hear that their minds and hearts were being poisoned by slavery. Indeed, he feared that what he said would only anger the white South and make it even more resistant to emancipation. Besides, to attack slavery publicly might cost him his political following. He never dropped his fear of being too advanced in his views, defending to his last days his policy of conciliation and delay. Like many leaders, he believed in the careful, step-by-step approach to the solving of social and political problems. (But if *he* could be patient, did he expect the slaves to be?)

Jefferson originally meant to have a few copies of the *Notes* printed in Philadelphia, but the cost was too high. In Paris he was able to publish it more cheaply. He had 200 copies printed, unsigned, circulating some to friends and asking them not to let it be made public. But once the book was out of his hands, he learned, unauthorized translations would surely follow unless he let his own version appear first. So the *Notes on Virginia* came out publicly at last, this time signed by the author. Although he kept minimizing its importance, the world treated it as a great contribution to human knowledge. John Adams wrote that "it will do its author and his country great honor. The passages upon slavery are worth diamonds. . . ."

No book that started out *not* to be one ever won its author so great a reputation as a scientist, a political thinker, and a man of letters.

With the approval of its president, he sent copies of the *Notes* to the students of the College of William and Mary. By now he doubted that his own generation would take action against slavery; it was to the young generation that he looked for the abolition of slavery, for they had "sucked in the principles of liberty with their mother's milk."

★ 10 ★

AN AMERICAN ABROAD

In his first winter in France as a diplomat, Jefferson found he had to contend with pirates. They preyed on shipping in the Mediterranean and even attacked the coastal towns. They took ships and cargoes, held captives for ransom, and enslaved those who couldn't pay for their freedom. They were based in the North African countries—Tunisia, Algeria, Morocco—where local rulers had made large-scale piracy their main source of revenue for centuries.

Several American ships and crews were taken captive even as he arrived in Paris. It enraged Jefferson, who felt helpless to prevent it. The British navy was able to protect its own shipping, but it was not interested in helping the upstart Americans.

Jefferson had authority to make treaties with the Barbary pirates, as they were called. To get their agreement, however, it would cost money, a great deal of it. Rather than pay bribes, he would prefer to win peace by armed force. He wrote home to urge that a navy be rapidly built, but Congress was not willing. Meanwhile more American ships were taken and the crews put to hard labor or jailed in chains.

To pay the ransom asked would cost large sums, but wouldn't going to war be even more expensive for America? Jefferson proposed instead that concerted action against the pirates be taken with those European powers who suffered from the raiders. His idea was ahead of its time. Each nation was out to gain the greatest advantage over all the others; they refused to cooperate. The Americans did succeed in making a deal for ransom with Morocco, but not with the other powers. The Barbary pirates would remain a constant problem for America, to be settled only when Jefferson became president.

Just as frustrating were Jefferson's persistent attempts to improve commerce between France and America. Many obstacles interfered. France herself faced bankruptcy. Her rigid bureaucracy barred attempts to change the way business was done, and those who profited from monopolistic practices protected the established system. Jefferson worked for a freer exchange of merchandise in the hope of opening markets for America's tobacco, whale oil, furs, rice, potash, beaver skins, leather, and wood. He managed to win some loosening of the regulations, but the concessions came to little when too many of the French ignored them.

In the spring of 1786 Jefferson found a chance to make a long-desired visit to England. He expected to stay only three weeks, but the trip extended to six. He came to London to help John Adams negotiate trade treaties with Portugal and Tripoli, as well as with Great Britain. They succeeded in arranging a treaty with the Portuguese minister, only to have his government reject it. Nor did bargaining with piratical Tripoli's man—who told them he believed making war on "sinners" was the duty of his people—achieve results.

As for England, a commercial treaty was hoped for because it would plainly be to mutual advantage. The British had products the Americans needed, and the United States had products the British needed and could get nowhere else.

So a deal made sense, except that Britain was still hostile to its lost colonies and showed contempt for a ramshackle America she expected would break apart any day. His experience in London strengthened Jefferson's belief that George III was a narrow-minded and stupid monarch and, like the English ruling class, arrogant and disdainful of the Americans. "Of all nations on earth," said Jefferson, "they require to be kicked into common good manners."

If it had not been for his great liking for John and Abigail Adams, his visit would have been most disappointing. What he did enjoy was his tour with Adams of English gardens, arranged in the informal style he preferred. He made precise notes on sixteen different ones he examined, looking for pointers he could apply at Monticello. English skill in making mechanical instruments he admired too, and bought a thermometer, protractor, globe telescope, botanical microscope, hygrometer, and theodolite. He also ordered a carriage, which took years to come, and a harpsichord.

While in England, Jefferson designed a portable copying press. This was an advance on a copying device created in 1780 by James Watt (inventor of the steam engine) which Jefferson had recently bought. By means of a rolling press it made possible the duplicating of writings. Jefferson had the portable press he designed made for him by a London craftsman and shipped to Paris. It eased the task of maintaining the files of his official papers as well as his outgoing personal correspondence. Later, when he became secretary of state, he introduced the practice of making multiple copies of documents for distribution, a procedure business firms as well as public agencies adopted.

Despite his dislike for the English, a feeling he never lost, he had to admit they were far advanced in the mechanical arts. Their artisans showed an enviable skill and patience in turning out excellent work. Observing the early stages of the industrial revolution, he admired especially the application of steam power to the operation of grist mills.

Back in Paris, Jefferson welcomed as a houseguest the young American painter Colonel John Trumbull, whom he had first met in London. The artist, a veteran of Washington's army, was planning to paint scenes from the Revolution, beginning with the signing of the Declaration of Independence. It was a project that appealed to Jefferson, who had already commissioned, on behalf of the Virginia legislature, a statue of General Washington. The sculptor was Jean-Antoine Houdon, one of Europe's finest, who would later do a bust of Jefferson.

Trumbull, quickly becoming part of Jefferson's circle, introduced two new arrivals in Paris, the fashionable painter Richard Cosway and his wife, Maria, an artist and musician herself. Busy with making miniature portraits commissioned by the French, Cosway, who was about Jefferson's age, left his young wife to be entertained by Jefferson and his friends. As soon as Jefferson, now forty-three, saw the twenty-seven-year-old Maria, he was intrigued by her as with no other woman since the death of his wife four years ago.

Young, well educated, lovely, Maria had been married for five years, but it was not a happy match. To Jefferson she had great appeal much like his wife's—"music, modesty, beauty, and that softness of disposition which is the ornament of her sex and the charm of ours." Her effect upon him was electrifying. He shed his cares and felt lighthearted for the first time in years. Part of her attractiveness was her complete indifference to politics, over which Jefferson thought ladies ought not to "wrinkle their foreheads." He made many excursions with her and their circle to the new artistic treasures of Paris and the nearby countryside. He was so in love that he felt his youth had been restored. And acting like an adolescent one day, he tried to leap over a fence, toppled to the ground, and dislocated his right wrist. It was poorly set and caused him much pain for years.

Early in October he saw the Cosways off to London and returned to his house "more dead than alive," as he wrote

Jefferson, painted by Matthew Brown in 1786, the year he fell in love with Maria Cosway

A miniature of Maria Cosway, painted by her husband. Below: A scene from Paris during Jefferson's time as minister to France.

her. With great difficulty, using his left hand, he sent Maria a twelve-page letter, one of the strangest to come from his pen. He wrote it in the form of "A Dialogue Between the Head and the Heart." The heart (emotion) voiced the happiness those days with Maria had given him. But the head (reason) warned of the danger of giving way to feelings that must cost him a great deal of pain and sorrow, for who knew how it would end? It would be sensible to try to forget her, and make a life alone once more, if he would avoid pain. And then the heart spoke again, reminding him of the great pleasure their romantic friendship had given him, worth any price he might pay. And he ended with the hope that she would return to Paris in the spring.

But it would be nearly a year before she saw him again in Paris. They exchanged many letters, his affectionate, hers warm too, but somewhat less encouraging than he had hoped. In one letter she guessed that the memory of a dead woman, Martha Jefferson, was her rival. And she asked if he meant to sit forever, "solitary and sad, on the beautiful Monticello tormented by the shadow of a woman. . . ." When she came in the late summer of 1787, she was alone: Why her husband did not come, we do not know. But the reunion was not what Jefferson had hoped for. They were rarely alone, and she was often away with the fashionable friends of a princess in whose home she was a guest. What had gone wrong? Perhaps Maria's difficulty in breaking away from a marriage, unhappy though it was, for she was a devout Catholic. Then too, she was wholly dependent on her husband for support. And perhaps she saw Jefferson more as a father than a lover; if he demanded more, she was uncertain what to do. The evidence for making a judgment is simply not there. She returned to England in December. Jefferson never saw her again.

But no sooner had Maria left than Trumbull introduced Jefferson to another charming (and married) woman, Mrs. Angelica Schuyler Church, newly arrived in Paris and a friend of Maria Cosway's. Jefferson was soon as romantically attached to Angelica. They spent much time together and he wrote her in the same playful, affectionate way; sometimes his letters to both were almost identical. When both women asked him for a miniature portrait, he had Trumbull paint one for each. Two months later, Angelica returned to England.

One can speculate that he needed such relationships with attractive women, but only when they were married. He could love them in the way he had loved his sister Jane, without violating the pledge he made at Martha's deathbed: that he would never marry again.

Early in 1787 Jefferson began what turned out to be the longest trip of his life. His object was to visit the south of France where, his doctor had advised, the mineral springs of Aix might strengthen his crippled wrist. Ever practical, he would combine the medical mission with study of the busy port of Marseilles to see what American shipping could learn from it. He also had little taste for the wintry wind and rain of Paris, and for its empty social life. This was a chance to escape all that.

He traveled in his own carriage, using post-horses and hiring servants at the longer stops. Along the way he saw the sights and dropped in at the chateaus of French noblemen to whom he had introductions. He was less interested in good company, however, than in acquiring knowledge of living conditions. He "courted the society of gardeners, vignerons, coopers, farmers," he said, and "devoted every moment of every day almost to the business of inquiry."

He was always comparing what he observed with his own Virginia. When he came upon the Maison Carrée, the ancient Roman building still standing at Nîmes, he gazed "whole hours at it," he said, like "a lover at his mistress." Before ever seeing it, except on paper, he had had a plaster model made and sent home, from which the Virginia State Capitol in Richmond was even now being constructed.

If the mineral waters at Aix did not help his wrist, at least the delicious climate pleased him. "I am now in the land of corn, wine, oil and sunshine," he wrote. "What more can a man ask of heaven? I am sure it will bring me to life again." He rode along the southern coast to Marseilles, where he heard that the Italians had a machine that cleaned rice better than those used in South Carolina. He decided to extend his trip and cross the Alps to see the machine in the rice fields of Lombardy.

The grandeur of the Alps overwhelmed him. Stopping briefly in Turin and in Milan, he was impressed by the enormous cathedrals, whose cost, he guessed, could have been put to much better use. He was more interested in looking over Italian agriculture. He recorded how their cheeses and wines were made and how the farm families worked and lived. Reaching the rice fields, he discovered that the cleaning machines were no better than the American ones; it was the species of rice that was different and superior. Although a death penalty threatened anyone who sent seed rice out of Italy, Jefferson paid a smuggler to carry a few sacks across the mountains and, to make sure some seeds would reach home, filled his own pockets with the best-quality rice. (Back in Paris, he shipped the rice to farmers he knew in South Carolina and Georgia.)

Early in May, after riding along the Italian Riviera, he was back in Marseilles. Here he wrote to Lafayette that the people he observed seemed to be working too many hours to pay the high rents the landlords demanded and to feed and clothe themselves. He urged the French nobleman to go out and visit the provinces himself, and to do it incognito, "to ferret the people out of their hovels as I have done, look into their kettles, eat their bread, loll on their beds . . . to find if they are soft."

Jefferson had his carriage placed on the deck of a barge, and made a nine-day journey on the canal connecting the Mediterranean with the Atlantic. He thought this kind of transport might prove useful in America. His notes of the 200-mile trip show how minutely he inspected the canal and its locks. As the barge was towed along slowly, he often stepped ashore to walk along the banks of the canal, viewing the olives, figs, mulberries, vines, corn, and pasture, as well as the villages and farms they passed by.

It was spring, and the nightingales were in full chorus in the trees bordering the canal. He wrote lyrically to his daughter Martha in Paris of the raptures their song sent him into. But he reported angrily on the hard work he saw women do on the canal. Most of the locks were kept by them, which required labor he thought much too heavy for women. They were also "the porters, carters, reapers, woodcutters, sailors, smiters on the anvil, cultivators of the earth. . . . Can we wonder if such of them as have a little beauty prefer easier courses to get their livelihood, as long as that beauty lasts?"

Reaching the Toulouse end of the canal, he drove to Bordeaux through wine country, making expert notes on every phase of wine production. He concluded that wine culture was not a good thing for land capable of growing anything else. Not that the French were drunks, no, but because those who worked in wine production were always poor. Yet he made himself a connoisseur of wine, and his fine taste would influence many others back home.

By the time he was back in Paris this man of science had piled up enough notes on landscape, climate, soil, plants, crops, bridges, boats, and the conditions of the working people to fill a book. He wrote a friend that he had "never passed three months and a half more delightfully." It is more useful to travel alone, he added, because it gives you the chance to reflect on what you see.

The long journey was typical of his unceasing efforts to enrich a mind that was already the best informed in America. What he learned of poverty and misery in France shocked him for its glaring contrast with the wealth of the aristocracy. Too few owned too much; too many had too little.

Could anything be done about it? He saw no practical way to bring about equal distribution of property. But, he suggested in a letter to James Madison, "a means of silently lessening the inequality of property is to exempt all from taxation below a certain point, and to tax the higher portions of property by geometrical progression as they rise."

And wasn't there something wrong, he wondered, in letting vast tracts of land in France go uncultivated while so many people were unemployed? If one believed, as he did, that "the earth is given as a common stock to man to labor and live on," then for great landlords to hang on to land without using it violated a natural right.

11

CONSTITUTION AT HOME, REVOLUTION IN FRANCE

Shortly after Jefferson's return to Paris his daughter Maria arrived from Virginia. Only four when her mother died, she had been living in Virginia with the Eppes family. When her father wrote for her to join him in France the child was unwilling to go. She would rather remain with her aunt and uncle and cousins in the home she loved than go to a strange country and a father and sister she hadn't seen for many years. But Jefferson refused to let her stay; he feared that to extend so long a separation from him and her sister would make them strangers for life.

In July the reluctant Maria arrived, in the company of her servant, fourteen-year-old Sally Hemings, a slave whose brother James had accompanied Jefferson to Paris. So much time had passed since Maria had last seen them that the nine-year-old did not recognize her father and sister. But they soon made her feel at home. She was placed in the convent school with Martha, now going on sixteen, and in a year was speaking French fluently.

The arrival of Maria made Jefferson happy, for he was very fond of children. He was easy in manner with young men too—nephews or the sons of friends—and enjoyed helping them all he could. Some he saw in Paris on their visits or during their schooling in Europe. Others he wrote to in America when they asked his advice. He would suggest reading lists, outline courses of study, recommend diet and exercise, help them when they were in financial trouble, and exchange with them news of events at home and abroad. Two of these young men, Jack Eppes and Thomas Mann Randolph, would marry his daughters.

Late in 1787 he learned he had been reelected minister to France for three more years. Soon after, John Adams wrote that he was leaving his London post to return home but first would go to the Netherlands to arrange loans for America. Jefferson decided to join him at the Hague in March. Their business settled successfully, Adams left him, and Jefferson made a two-week trip up the Rhine to Strasbourg, and then by carriage through Alsace, Lorraine, and the Champagne countryside. He relished the romantic scenery but was appalled by the poverty he observed in Prussia, and the "slave-like fear" he saw in the faces of the people, which he attributed to living under a monarchy's domination.

He noted how intolerant one religion was of another. Where Catholics were in the majority, they oppressed the Protestants, and where Lutherans were dominant, they made trouble for the Catholics and Calvinists.

Never ignoring practical matters, he made notes on the mechanical arts, population, architecture, and agriculture wherever he went. In one place he watched plowmen behind their oxen and noticed how awkward their moldboard was. Couldn't there be a better design? He promptly made rough sketches of one. When he returned to America he would perfect a moldboard that earned him great prestige both in Europe and America.

It was while Jefferson was serving in France that an event occurred at home which made the Founding Fathers tremble. Civil war broke out in western Massachusetts. Poor farmers, home from fighting the Revolution, were deep in debt to merchants because the Congress had failed to pay their soldiers' wages. The veterans feared the courts would foreclose on their homes and farms. Led by Captain Dan Shays, 1,500 men besieged the courts to prevent them from sitting and broke into jails to free persons held for debt. The frightened judges promised to do nothing until the veterans' grievances were settled.

News of Shays' Rebellion angered Washington and other national leaders. Did this mean a government of the people would end only in anarchy? If the uprising spread, how could the weak Congress, which had no funds and no army, put it down?

When word of the uprising finally reached Jefferson in Paris, he was jolted. He didn't expect the independent farmers he took such pride in to fight against their own government. He feared their action would have a harmful effect on the European powers, all too ready to believe in the collapse of America. His feelings were mixed. He didn't like to see citizens interfere with the orderly processes of the courts or to try to settle their grievances by resorting to force. But neither did he want the veterans to be punished.

The rebellion ended when the governor of Massachusetts sent 4,000 state militiamen to prevent an attack by Shays' men upon the U.S. arsenal at Springfield. In a brief skirmish four rebels were killed and the rest surrendered on the promise of a pardon. Jefferson wrote to Abigail Adams that he hoped the promise would be kept. "The spirit of resistance to government is so valuable on certain occasions, that I wish it to be always kept alive. It will often be exercised when wrong, but better so than not to be exercised at all. I like a little rebellion now and then. It is like a storm in the atmosphere."

In a letter to another friend he wrote some famous lines that are always being quoted: "I hold it that a little rebellion now and then is a good thing. . . . It is a medicine neces-

When Shays' men attacked the Springfield arsenal, Jefferson was in France. He thought this "little rebellion" to be a "good thing" to preserve the spirit of liberty.

sary for the sound health of government. . . . God forbid that we should ever be twenty years without a rebellion. . . . The tree of liberty must be refreshed from time to time with the blood of patriots and tyrants. It is its natural manure."

It was Shays' Rebellion that gave support to men who saw the need to strengthen the American government. At Philadelphia on May 25, 1787, a convention of fifty-five delegates met to draft a constitution that would meet the needs of the Union better than the old Articles of Confederation.

The delegates worked in secret, thinking it wise to argue out their differences behind closed doors and then to submit their conclusions to the nation. Jefferson thought this secrecy an "abominable" precedent. Despite his great experience in lawmaking and his deep interest in principles of good government, he could do little from this distance to help. The best he could do was to send Madison, a prime mover in the convention, several books on ancient and modern government which might provide clues as to how a federal republic could be shaped.

He also offered his own views. Like Madison he believed in separation of powers and in a government with checks and balances. If the legislative, executive, and judicial branches would have equal but different powers, then power would not be concentrated in any one branch. Thus the growth of tyranny would be prevented.

The delegates finished their draft in mid-September, but it was months before Jefferson received a copy of the proposed constitution. His first reaction was about fifty-fifty: "There are very good articles in it," he said, "and very bad. I do not know which preponderate."

Two things he did not like above all. One was the omission of a Bill of Rights. He believed it was vital to impose restraints on the federal government so that it would not abuse the rights of the individual. Among the rights he insisted on protecting were freedom of religion and of the press, and trial by jury. His other complaint was the lack of any limit on the number of terms a president might serve. Without such a restriction couldn't a president be reelected repeatedly and hold office for life? That smacked of monarchy.

After Madison wrote him in detail how the debates in the convention had gone, he felt more favorable to the Constitution. He hoped the states would ratify it but with a demand that a Bill of Rights be added quickly as amendments. And that is what happened. It was only the promise of a Bill of Rights that finally settled the outcome of the heated debates on the Constitution in the states. By June 21, 1788, the necessary nine states had ratified, and the Constitution was now in effect.

The debates over the Constitution and their final resolution by peaceful agreement gave Jefferson reason to feel proud of the new republic. He felt the despotic nations of Europe had something to learn from the intelligent way a self-governing society functioned. "The example of changing a constitution by assembling the wise men of the State, instead of assembling armies," he wrote, "will be worth as much to the world as the former examples we had given them." The Constitution itself, he believed, was "the wisest ever yet presented" to the world.

At the same time the Constitution was being written, events in France were moving rapidly. Her revolution began as an effort to reform an arbitrary monarchy weakened by debt and corrupt administration. Under great pressure the government was at last permitting freedom of criticism. Jefferson saw political posters appear on the walls and political caricatures in the press. "In the course of three months," he wrote Adams, "the royal authority has lost, and the rights of the nation gained, as much ground, by a revolution of public opinion only, as England gained in all her civil wars under the Stuarts."

He had no way of knowing what a violent, a bloody end this would come to as demands for social justice outran the initial attempts at moderate, constitutional reform. The "gay and thoughtless Paris" he had deplored was now "a furnace of politics." With Lafayette and other friends among the French intellectuals, he discussed the speedy turn of events. The loyalty of the army was in doubt, and some leaders were calling for a declaration of rights.

In the summer and fall of 1788 he saw riots in the streets and the killing of demonstrators by Paris guards. Martial law was imposed and the government summoned a National Assembly to meet early in 1789. Jefferson thought the king's desperate need for money would open the way for a peaceful evolution into constitutional monarchy. He argued with his French friends for gradual change, fearful that proposals too radical would provoke the forces of conservatism to take up arms. Optimistically, he trusted the aristocracy to accept reforms which others closer to power said they would never do.

It is hard for us today to think ourselves back into that time and place. We take popular sovereignty, civil liberty, equality before the law for granted. We can't imagine how explosive such ideas were to the French in 1789. Most people, living for centuries under the old feudal regime, assumed that people were unequal, that inequality was a good thing, that in fact it was ordained by God Himself. Say "liberty" to the French whom Jefferson observed, and it meant only special privileges denied to other persons. The king, the source of law, decided who deserved privilege. It was his right as the annointed representative of God on earth.

When a period of relative calm set in, Jefferson asked for permission to return home for a six-month leave of absence. After some five years in France he needed to look after his estates and to return his daughters to their native Virginia. Besides, sixteen-year-old Martha was thinking of turning Catholic and becoming a nun, a prospect he did not like.

Because his request arrived when the American government was busy shifting from the old Articles to the new Constitution, no action was taken till August of 1789. That kept him in Paris at a time when the most dramatic events occurred. In the bitterly cold winter of 1788–89 he saw the government desperately scrambling for money, the people starving for bread and freezing for lack of fuel, and the masses of unemployed clamoring for work.

Lafayette and his friends were trying their hands at framing declarations of rights, taking what Jefferson and the Americans had done as their inspiration. Ignoring the rules of diplomatic behavior, Jefferson met with them to give advice and share his insights. The collapse of a whole social order was close; he watched the French struggle to find some form of order in the chaos surrounding them. The possibilities seemed limitless, both for good and for evil. Some dreamed of creating a utopia; others feared France would fall back into tyranny.

On July 14, 1789, the people of Paris stormed the fortress called the Bastille. The violence had begun: 150 people were killed or injured in the attack upon the Bastille, and when the mob seized its governor, they cut off his head and paraded it through the city on the end of a pike. Jefferson went to watch the Bastille torn down stone by stone, and later sent funds to the women whose husbands had died in its capture. Princes, aristocrats, and ministers fled the country. The king gave in to the popular will and conceded some reforms. Jefferson rejoiced, but as the peasants rose up in the provinces, burned chateaus, and began to execute officials, he observed that "their hatred is stronger than their love."

When the Assembly adopted a Declaration of Rights late in August, he called it the "death certificate of the Old Regime," and a promise that his cherished liberty of the mind and conscience would be fully realized in the future.

Jefferson saw the vast upheaval he had lived through in the American Revolution occurring to another people. The circumstances were different, but underlying the two revolutions was the conviction that ordinary people could make history, not just suffer it. When things fall apart people can respond to an overwhelming need to make sense of life by rebuilding society on new principles. In America, those principles were life, liberty, and the pursuit of happiness. And in France, liberty, equality, fraternity.

It was Jefferson's duty to report objectively on the revolutionary developments. Through Lafayette's circle and his official role he was in a good position to gather the facts. He sent John Jay, the American minister of foreign affairs, his

Parisians storm the Bastille on July 14, 1789. Jefferson witnessed this event.

view that while civil war in France was possible, he was optimistic that Lafayette's party would be able to save the situation.

In October, Jefferson and his daughters, with James and Sally Hemings, left for America. He took aboard boxes of books for Washington, Franklin, and Madison, small trees and plants he would transplant at home, wines, cheeses, clothes, pictures, books, harpsichord, guitar, and his old carriage.

In his five years in France he had grown fond of "this great and good country." If he had to live somewhere else than in America, he said, France would be the country of his choice.

Late in November their ship docked at Norfolk. Before leaving for Monticello, Jefferson learned that President Washington had nominated him to be secretary of state and that the Senate had confirmed the nomination. While he had been away, Congress had combined foreign affairs and domestic administration (except for defense and finance) into one department under the secretary of state. He wrote the president that he would rather remain minister to France but would like a few months to think it over.

Then he climbed into his carriage and headed for home.

★ 12 ★

AT PRESIDENT WASHINGTON'S SIDE

Riding home through Virginia, Jefferson "was astonished at the change" he observed. The people were so different from the way he remembered them: "their notions, their habits and manner, the course of their commerce, so totally changed. . . ." He felt how remote he had become from his Virginians in these years away from home. Yet they had not forgotten him. At Monticello he and his daughters received a grand welcome. "Wild with joy," all his slaves had been given the day off to celebrate the master's homecoming. As his party came in view the slaves crowded around the carriage, shouting and cheering him all the way to the door. Years later Martha wrote she had never witnessed such an outpouring of affection.

His first obligation was to decide what to do about the cabinet post offered him. He had told Madison that he wanted to retire from office, and especially any that would require him to remain away from home a long time. But his admiration for Washington made him hesitate to refuse him. On the other hand, when he looked about him at Virginia's primitive little towns, her immense stretches of dark forest, and her meager cultural life, he thought longingly of the sophisticated Paris he could return to and the turbulent revolution it would be a pity to miss observing.

While he brooded over the decision, he rode across his lands to see what needed attention. The plantations had failed to produce a profit in his absence; he would have to borrow money to meet debts. He planted what he had carried from France and saw to necessary repairs. Evenings he read or played the violin, or Martha, at the piano, would accompany friends in song.

Three months after his return home, Martha married Thomas Mann Randolph, Jr., the son of the Randolph that Jefferson had lived with in Tuckahoe until he was nine. The young man, now twenty-one, was a cousin of Martha's, but inbreeding in the gentry was common then. Jefferson approved of the marriage: he thought Martha's love was "a young gentleman of genius, science, and honorable mind." The groom's father promised him a plantation with forty slaves, and Jefferson gave Martha 1,000 acres of forest land and twenty-five slaves. About a year later the couple gave Jefferson his first grandchild, named Anne Cary. They also began giving him much to worry about, for his son-in-law proved to be a poor manager of affairs. Still, when trouble arose, Jefferson was always there to straighten things out.

Meanwhile President Washington had grown impatient. He asked Madison to ride over to Monticello and press his friend for an answer. Jefferson was confident he could handle the nation's foreign affairs. But to have a huge mass of *domestic* problems also dumped in his lap? Any mistakes he might make in handling them would surely invite public criticism. He was extremely sensitive to the opinions of others, a trait in a politician that can be disastrous. Finally, on February 14, 1790, after still other prominent men added their pressure, he accepted the task, telling himself that as soon as he could do it decently, he would quit.

Federal Hall in New York City, the seat of the U.S. government when Jefferson served in Washington's cabinet

He left the plantations in the care of his overseer, with his son-in-law assisting. Mary was put in Martha's hands. On March 21 he arrived in New York City, the nation's capital at the time, and reported to President Washington. He learned his salary would be $3,500 a year, much less than he estimated his living expenses would be. He found a house at 57 Maiden Lane, which he made both home and offices. He brought with him household slaves, footmen, and a coachman. To live in his accustomed comfort required the best furniture, good wine, French cooking, and a carriage and horses.

By the time Jefferson joined the cabinet, Washington had been in office nearly a year. The changeover from the old Confederation Congress to the new constitutional gov-

President Washington, at right, with his first cabinet: Henry Knox, seated; next to him stands Jefferson; Edmund Randolph, seen from the back; and Alexander Hamilton.

ernment was well under way. The president had moved carefully, knowing his decisions would set the direction and character of government for a long time to come.

The first major business to be completed was adoption of the Bill of Rights to keep the promises made to assure ratification of the Constitution. In those early months the government enjoyed the fullest support from both the Congress and the people. But as Jefferson arrived on the scene, the honeymoon had begun to fade.

Differences sprang up, inevitably. For America was then—and even more so now—a nation of diverse peoples and interests. Many social, economic, and regional groups, as well as ethnic and racial groups, make competing demands on the government. So conflict is inevitable. A democratic government's job is to mediate those varying demands, ideally with the public benefit in mind. But the ideal is rarely if ever achieved. Politics comes down to a power struggle over the distribution of society's goods, and short of revolution, the struggle is settled by negotiation.

When Washington was elected president it was by unanimous choice. Everyone agreed the Revolution's leader had to be the one to launch the new republic. No political parties existed at the time. The Constitution made no provision for them. The Founding Fathers distrusted parties and called them factions, groups out to grab control of affairs. Parties, they thought, would invite corruption. Why couldn't citizens vote for candidates without party labels? Men like themselves, upper class mostly, who would agree on what was best for the entire nation.

It didn't work out that way. Various groups were bound to clash over many issues and for different reasons. Those who knew what they wanted saw that a strong federal government would make important decisions affecting the interests of every group, for good or bad. The conflict was crystallized in the two figures who dominated Washington's cabinet: Jefferson, secretary of state, and Hamilton, secretary of the treasury. They took leadership in the political battle over whose interests the government would serve. Hamilton, a financial wizard, spoke for the well-to-do conservatives called the Federalists. This was a dangerous world for a struggling new nation, he said. To survive it had to be strong and energetic. It needed solid finances and a good name among Europe's money men. He foresaw America's potential as an economic power and was determined to promote its growth. Encouraging manufacturing at home and trade abroad, he said, was the best way to build national wealth. And the surest path to that end was free enterprise, or competitive self-interest, both for the nation and for the individual.

While Hamilton was forward-looking in economics, he was deeply conservative in politics. He had shown at the Constitutional Convention in Philadelphia how much he distrusted the ordinary citizen. "The people," he said, "are turbulent and changing; they seldom judge or determine right." He wanted power centered in the wealthy, so they could hold the reins on the unsteady people. He even argued that both the Senate and the president should be elected for life.

Now, in a series of major reports to the Congress, Hamilton outlined a program to stabilize the government's finances and establish its credit, to promote commerce abroad and economic development at home, and to make the foundation of foreign policy a commercial and diplomatic alliance with England.

Hamilton's policies favored the moneyed seaboard class, while leaving the agricultural South pretty much to shift for itself. But working people in the northern towns and cities liked his program too. Expansion of commerce and manufacturing would provide jobs for them. So long as their own economic condition improved, they didn't worry about the special benefits that his money and banking policy would bring to the few.

Jefferson took the lead in opposing many of Hamilton's

projects. He came from a farming society, hostile to radical changes. He too supported the extension of the nation across the continent, but he thought it would take hundreds of years. Yes, he wanted Americans to grow more prosperous, but the way his class of Virginians did, by shaping their own lives, with as little interference from government, state or national, as possible. He did not like economic activity that would draw masses of people to huddle in great cities, corrupters of man's morals, health, and liberties. He spoke for the anti-Federalists, the southern planters and the small farmers of all regions who saw the government was helping business by generous credit while giving themselves no relief from debt and taxation. They felt threatened by the power of the "ins," the Federal Party. Jefferson viewed Hamilton as a monarchist at heart, a dangerous reactionary. Jefferson was suspicious of the business class and did not want to see monopoly and special favors granted to the powerful class Hamilton represented.

To carry out his duties Jefferson had precious little help. For the State Department's entire staff—only two chief clerks, two assistant clerks, and a translator—the budget was $4,500, not including Jefferson's own salary. Washington was very much in charge of his cabinet. He viewed them as assistants who required his approval for all major decisions. Early on, he sent Jefferson to testify before a Senate committee on how the State Department was going to operate. Present was Senator William Maclay, whose diary entry for that day in May 1790 lets us see how Jefferson appeared to one of his contemporaries:

> Jefferson is a slender man. Has rather an air of stiffness in his manner. His clothes seem too small for him. He sits in a lounging manner on one hip, commonly, with one of his shoulders elevated much above the other. His face has a scrawny aspect. His whole figure has a loose shackling air. He had

> a rambling vacant look and nothing of that firm collected deportment which I expected would dignify the presence of a Secretary or Minister. I looked for gravity, but a laxity of manner seemed shed about him. He spoke almost without ceasing. But even his discourse partook of his personal demeanor. It was loose and rambling and yet he scattered information wherever he went, and some even brilliant sentiments sparkled from him.

One of Jefferson's first duties was to draft a plan for establishing a uniform national system of weights and measures. After six months of intense study he handed Congress an elaborate plan for a decimal system. But, as an alternative, he proposed that the existing system—which varied much from state to state—be redefined, made uniform, and introduced only gradually. Congressional committees discussed the plan for six years without any legislation being adopted. It took several decades before standards were established.

Soon after, Hamilton's proposals on how to fund the national debt and handle the debts incurred by the colonies during the Revolution produced a deadlock in Congress. Hamilton's plan, the opposition felt, would put millions in the pockets of a small group of speculators who had bought up obligations of soldiers, farmers, and small businessmen for as little as five cents on the dollar. The money to pay for this handout would come from taxation of all the people. The goal of putting the nation on a stable paying basis was sound. It was the way Hamilton wanted to do it that caused an uproar.

As Jefferson and Hamilton tried to find a means of breaking the deadlock, a way opened up. For some time the Congress had been arguing over where to place the permanent capital of the government. Northerners favored New York or Philadelphia; Southerners wanted a site on the Potomac. Each region wished to keep federal power close to its own economic center. Putting these two issues together, Hamilton and Jefferson worked out a political deal. The Treasury chief would line up northern votes to locate the capital in the South, while the State Department chief would line up southern votes to adopt Hamilton's economic proposal. (It was agreed that the government would remain in Philadelphia for ten years, when the new "Federal City" should be ready.) Two years later, as his differences with Hamilton became more intense, Jefferson regretted that he had been "made a tool for forwarding his schemes."

Before his first year of service was up, Jefferson faced issues of foreign policy that generated powerful feelings. And here too, Hamilton split with him over how to deal with the European powers England and France. London had tightened its controls over U.S. trade. Jefferson's ally Madison got Congress to pass bills threatening any nation with commercial retaliation for treating American trade unfairly. The bills favored U.S. ships in American ports and imposed import duties on foreign goods entering the country. Because France bought more than it sold to America, the bills were thought to favor French trade.

Hamilton opposed this policy. His plans for strengthening the American economy required a great deal of money. Those sums had to come from land sales or import taxes on goods that were mostly British. He disliked any measure that would threaten England and might lead to the cutting off of British loans and investments, or even to war. So he worked against any attempt to get tough with Britain, even conniving secretly with the British minister to thwart Jefferson's plans. Of course his opposition infuriated the secretary of state.

A crisis erupted when Spanish naval officers foolishly seized British ships off America's northwest coast. London said it would retaliate by marching troops from Canada down through the Mississippi Valley to conquer Spanish colonies along the Caribbean. If they did that, it would place British power on all four sides of the United States, surrounding her, in effect. We mustn't let them make that march, Jefferson advised Washington. Hamilton, however, advised doing nothing to antagonize the British. Luckily, before Washington had to take action, the Spanish backed down and apologized for the ship seizures. The crisis was over.

Not all Jefferson's attention went to foreign affairs. Besides preparing the report on weights and measures he had the job of issuing patents on inventions. The nation's first Patent Law was passed only weeks after he took office, outlining how inventors must apply for protection of their creations. He didn't welcome this task, but was pleased by how rapidly American genius began to emerge because of the protection given it. He approved sixty-seven applications of the far greater number submitted during his years as secretary of state. With no Patent Office yet in place, it piled a great burden on his already overloaded shoulders.

Sometimes Jefferson had to do more than simply read the plans and examine the models handed in by inventors. If necessary, he personally tested the invention. Once, for example, he investigated a claim by a Rhode Island man that he had developed a new method for distilling potable water from salt water by means of a new apparatus. If the process worked, it would be invaluable to ships at sea and to castaway sailors. Jefferson called on several scientists to conduct experiments testing the invention and then submitted a report to the Congress based not only on their findings (positive) but on his own scholarly research into all attempts to achieve the same goal from the sixteenth century on. The Congress issued his report, making it the first scientific paper to be published under government auspices.

The other major project handed to Jefferson's office was supervision of the Residence Act of 1790. This was the outcome of his compromise with Hamilton calling for establishing a new permanent seat of government within the next ten years along the Potomac River. The exact site was to be chosen by President Washington. Jefferson was closely involved with every phase: selecting the territory, acquiring the property, designing a new city in the wilderness. Only his experience and skills, exercised in close cooperation with the president, could have made it a success. A 10-mile-square piece of land was acquired for the site, called the District of Columbia. At the center of the square the Federal City was laid out, soon known as "Washington." The city plan was made by Major Pierre Charles L'Enfant and Andrew Ellicott. It was the first city in the world specially created as a national capital.

Jefferson had learned a great deal about foreign architecture in his years abroad and had collected many plans of European cities and their important buildings. He gave L'Enfant his plans and advised him on the design of both the Capitol building and the White House. He suggested that the streets be wide, straight, and spacious, laid out at right angles, and bordered by trees. It was L'Enfant who added to Jefferson's rectangular street pattern the series of radiating spaced circles. Despite the inevitable quarrels between architects and sponsors, the city of Washington was finally ready for occupancy by the government in 1799. Sadly, by the time it was built, Washington himself was dead. He was the only president never to live in what came to be called the White House.

With Congress recessed, Jefferson made a trip home to Monticello. Returning to Philadelphia, he rented a three-story house on Market near 8th Street. Although he expected to be there for only a few years, he made expensive changes to suit his desire for comfort and conveniences. He had a room added to house his large library, another structure to hold three carriages, and a stable for five horses. Soon seventy-eight crates arrived from France, with furniture, books, clocks, stoves, tableware, vases, kitchen utensils, a dozen cases of wine, and even a case of macaroni. It took months to unpack everything; the house became livable only after the efficient maître d'hôtel who had served him in Paris arrived to take charge.

Jefferson did most of his official work in his home, which was only a few blocks from the president's house and close by the meeting place of Congress. Evidence of his immense productivity is in the fact that in the three months of the First Congress's final session he completed a major report nearly every week.

A key measure before Congress was Hamilton's proposal for a national bank. It would issue currency and help carry on the nation's financial affairs. All federal taxes would be deposited in the bank, whose directors could invest that money. A fifth of the bank's stock would be owned by the government, and four-fifths by private citizens. Since a majority of the stockholders would elect the bank's directors, control of the bank's affairs would be in the hands of private citizens.

Congress passed the bill with little debate. Jefferson and Madison, however, strongly objected to it, and urged the president to veto the bill. They said the bank would have too much power over the country's economy. They also said, just as importantly, that it was unconstitutional.

Why? Because the Constitution did not specifically authorize such a national bank. Jefferson cited the Tenth Amendment (part of the Bill of Rights), which states that "all powers not delegated to the United States . . . are reserved to the states, or to the people." That means, he claimed, that the government has *only* those powers specifically listed in the Constitution. His literal interpretation of the Constitution came to be known as "strict construction."

Hamilton, taking the other side, favored a loose construction of the Constitution. The government, he said, has more powers than are actually listed. And he cited Section 8, Clause 18 of the Constitution, which gives Congress the power to make all laws "necessary and proper" to carry out the powers that are listed in the Constitution. He argued that because the government has the power to tax, then it also has the power to create a bank to hold those taxes.

Both men gave Washington their opinions in written documents. Washington decided in favor of Hamilton.

Hamilton's position came to be known as the doctrine of "implied powers." The concept probably should be credited to Madison, not Hamilton. The Treasury chief borrowed it to suit his own immediate purpose. The issue of strict versus liberal interpretation of the Constitution has been debated by the courts and among the people right down to today. Whenever a new Supreme Court justice is to be appointed, the question is asked, which view does the candidate take?

★ 13 ★

PARTISAN POLITICS

Before Washington's first term ended, the seeds of what would become political parties were firmly planted. In the popular mind Jefferson and Hamilton symbolized the opposing sides. Each side, Federalist or anti-Federalist, would treat the other as a bitter enemy. And both would quickly use the slogans, catchphrases and stereotypes that have characterized political parties ever since. Neither party, in these early years, drew broad public participation. The direction of party policy would be in the hands of only a few people, on both state and national levels.

After the national-bank issue was settled in Hamilton's favor Jefferson with his friend Madison left Philadelphia for a trip into upstate New York and western New England. With Congress adjourned, this would be a chance for the Virginians to see new country and relax. But Jefferson always had to make his trips useful; he kept careful notes on scenery, plants, industry, farming, mileage (920 all told), and the quality of inns they stayed at. They visited Revolutionary battlefields, caught trout and bass in Lake George, killed two rattlesnakes, and shot three red squirrels. They returned through the Berkshires, down the Connecticut River, crossed the Sound, and rode the north shore of Long Island to New York City.

A pleasure trip, yes, but a political mission too. In New York State a few families were struggling for control of state politics. Governor George Clinton and Aaron Burr led one side, and the Schuylers, related to Hamilton by marriage, controlled the other. Jefferson and Madison seem to have formed an alliance with the Clinton-Burr faction during the trip. It marked a turning point in national politics. The leaders of two powerful states, Virginia and New York, were moving toward founding a national party of opposition.

Another major step taken was to establish a press supporting their point of view. At the time, the one influential newspaper in Philadelphia, the nation's capital, was John Fenno's *Gazette of the United States.* It always backed Hamilton and his policies and relied on printing contracts from the Treasury Department and personal loans from Hamilton.

Jefferson found an able editor to launch a newspaper on his behalf. He appointed the poet Philip Freneau to an undemanding clerkship in his State Department, and Freneau started the *National Gazette* in the fall of 1791. He filled its columns with praise for Jefferson and attacks upon Hamilton.

It helped Freneau mightily that Jefferson gave him access to much material in the State Department files, access granted to no other editors. (Perhaps the earliest example of a government official "leaking" news.) As Freneau's savaging of Federalist people and policies continued, Washington wanted the editor restrained in some way. But Jefferson said no, his paper was saving the country from "galloping fast into monarchy." While that fear was exaggerated, Freneau's paper did prove itself to be a powerful promoter of Republican views and of Jefferson himself as the champion of every anti-Federalist.

Charles Willson Peale painted the two rivals in Washington's cabinet: Alexander Hamilton, secretary of treasury, left, and Jefferson, secretary of state.

By the time the Second Congress met in the fall of 1791 two opposing groups were clearly forming in the national legislature. Not yet political parties in any formal sense, they spread the ideas of their leaders from the forum of the capital to the broad public beyond.

During the heated newspaper quarrels the Jeffersonians damned the opposition with such names as aristocrats, monarchists, speculators, Tories, while the Hamiltonians borrowed a term from the French Revolution and called the enemy "Jacobins," meaning bloody extremists.

For what had happened in France was that civil war had broken out. Those, like Lafayette, who had hoped for a constitutional monarchy, lost out, with the government taken over by the more radical Jacobin wing. They got rid of the monarchy and beheaded the king. Declaring France a republic, they began a military crusade to destroy monarchy and privilege throughout Europe.

In America, conservatives saw in this change only bloodshed and anarchy. But large crowds took to the streets to demonstrate their support of the French Revolution. They cheered at the news of the king's beheading. Liberals believed the freedom of all humanity was at stake. Many defended the Revolution, and some, even the terror which destroyed thousands in the name of the collective good of the people.

Jefferson himself defended what was going on in France with such statements as: "We are not to be expected to be translated from despotism to liberty, in a feather-bed." When his protégé William Short criticized the Jacobins, Jefferson wrote him that:

> The liberty of the whole earth was depending on the issue of the contest, and was ever such a prize won with so little innocent blood? My own affections have been deeply wounded by some of the martyrs of this cause, but rather than it should have

Louis XVI of France was beheaded by the guillotine in 1793. Despite the terror, most Americans favored the French Revolution.

failed I would have seen half the earth desolated; were there but an Adam and Eve left in every country, and left free, it would be better than as it now is.

That is a horrifying vision of mass extermination as a means of wiping out inequality. As the world has seen many times since Jefferson, this "cure" for injustice only perpetuates the evil it is intended to eliminate.

The Federalists were alarmed. They feared what American mobs might do against the rich and powerful here if the contagion spread. When Hamilton's press denounced the demonstrators supporting the French Revolution as "filthy Jacobins," they only hooted and began to organize Jacobin clubs and call one another "Citizen" in the French manner.

Jefferson took a month's vacation at Monticello and brought Mary back to Philadelphia with him so she could go to a nearby school where he could see her often. He was distressed by the poor crops gathered at his plantations and over his inability to pay his large debts and those of his sister and nephews. Finally he had to sell not only one of his plantations but a considerable number of his slaves. Still, he kept on spending to maintain a lavish style of living. He ordered 500 bottles of the best French wine, a set of costly drawings, a new coat, and three pairs of silk-and-satin breeches. Nor did he halt work on a major construction project at Monticello.

Early in 1792 he told Washington he'd like to resign. The paper work seemed endless, the results of his labors hard to judge, and the political climate distasteful. He longed to return to peaceful rural life. The "fine sunshine" of Albemarle, he wrote a neighbor, "seems made for all the world but me." The president wouldn't hear of resignation. He valued both Hamilton and Jefferson too highly to want to do without them. But dismayed by their mounting antagonism, he appealed to the two rivals to settle their differences and work together for the public good. Each man defended his position, both saying they wanted to cooperate with their chief. But Hamilton continued writing anonymous pieces for Fenno's paper, trying to force Jefferson to quit.

The second presidential election loomed ahead. Washington was sixty now and felt these political battles were too much, piled on top of the daily pressures of his office. The constant attacks on his government angered him. He told the cabinet he would not run for reelection. They urged him to continue in office: his authority was needed to strengthen the national government. Jefferson argued that only Washington could protect the Union from the arrogant Federalists; Hamilton argued Washington was needed to hold off the fanatical Republicans.

At last Washington agreed to hold on for another term, hoping his presence would prevent the political split from getting deeper. Both parties pledged to support him, and no one ran against him.

But the Republicans saw the office of the vice presidency as fair game. They set to work to replace John Adams. They thought some of the things he was saying lately tended away from democracy and toward monarchy. So the New York–Virginia alliance created a Republican opposition and put up New York's Governor Clinton for the office. There was still no formal party organization, but in every state small groups of Jeffersonians nominated congressional candidates and began to build a strong party. In the end Adams beat out Clinton. Still, Jefferson was pleased that in the House of Representatives the new party had come close to taking control.

Early in 1793 France declared war against England. It sharpened immensely the division of Americans. Jefferson saw it as an old enemy fighting an old friend. France had helped America powerfully in her War for Independence, and America still had an alliance with her. Should France be helped in her struggle against the allied monarchs of Europe?

The Federalists, on the other hand, were anti-French because it suited their economic interests. Merchants did most of their trading with England. And war would increase the business if America would remain neutral. Hamilton feared that support of the French Revolution might bring on war with Britain. And that would mean economic disaster, for most of America's imports came from Britain.

In July, Jefferson handed Washington his resignation, to take effect in September. Once again the president insisted he postpone leaving until the year's end. The secretary of state's troubles increased when Edmond Genêt, the new French minister, began maneuvers here which embarrassed the Jeffersonians. He organized pro-French clubs that loudly criticized America's neutrality policy. Washington demanded that Jefferson stop this interference and have Genêt recalled; Jefferson had to agree that the man's behavior was intolerable. But before anyone could act, Genêt's friends in Paris lost power and he was ordered home. Fearing the guillotine, he quit public life and stayed in America.

While Genêt's intrigues cost France many friends in America, the British too were losing supporters here. Her navy had begun to stop American ships and seize sailors. Claiming they were British deserters, the officers forced them into the royal navy. Britain had also failed to withdraw from northern forts in the United States, which she had agreed to do by treaty ten years earlier. And now she was charged with selling weapons to Native Americans who were battling to keep white invaders off their lands.

From France the American minister, Gouverneur Morris, wrote Jefferson to ask what policy toward the revolutionary government should be. Jefferson replied: "It accords with our principles to acknowledge any government to be rightful which is formed by the will of the nation substantially declared. . . . We surely cannot deny to any nation that right whereon our own government is founded, that every one may govern itself under whatever forms it pleases, and change these forms at its own will. . . ."

Despite his sympathy for the French in the war with England, Jefferson, like Hamilton, advised that the United States should remain neutral: "We wish not to meddle with the internal affairs of any country, nor with the general affairs of Europe. Peace with all nations, and the right which that gives us with respect to all nations, are our object."

In April, the president issued a Proclamation of Neutrality. Madison blasted the president for exercising a power that Madison asserted belonged to Congress. For if a president could declare neutrality, then could he not also decide whether and against whom the United States might declare war? And it was only to Congress that the Constitution gave that power. But Washington stuck to his policy and established a precedent that claimed important power for the president.

A plague of yellow fever swept Philadelphia that summer. Everybody who could, fled the capital. Jefferson went to his office every day until mid-September, when the president left for Mount Vernon. Then the secretary of state departed for Monticello. When the epidemic passed in November, it left 5,000 dead. The Congress and the cabinet returned to continue business. Jefferson took up his last obligation in office—a report for Congress on American commerce overseas. In it he supported the principle of free trade—that "every country be employed in producing that which nature has best fitted it to produce, and each be free to exchange with others the mutual surpluses for mutual wants." That was the ideal goal; meanwhile he called for a policy of reciprocity—that is, making deals with other nations where possible, and imposing restrictions when negotiations failed.

On the last day of 1793 Jefferson formally resigned his office. In a few days, he was on his way to Monticello.

14

LIFE AT MONTICELLO

It took Jefferson ten days to travel the 300 miles between Philadelphia and Monticello. No matter, for he was home at last and meant never to travel again. For the next three years he scarcely stirred except for one trip to Richmond. It was family that this fifty-year-old grandfather valued above all: "The most solid of all earthly happiness is of the domestic kind, in a well-assorted family, all the members of which set a just value on each other, and are disposed to make the happiness of each other their first object."

Living with him at Monticello were his daughters, Maria, now fifteen, Martha, twenty-one, her husband Thomas Mann Randolph, Jr., and their two babies, a boy and a girl. Jefferson's affection for his family was expressed in generous aid to any who were in need. It included his sisters and their families as well, and went beyond to other people he was not obligated to but for his sympathy for those in trouble. Sometimes he was made the victim of false appeals but he thought that to be miserly was worse than to be gullible.

This, although his financial condition when he left office was anything but good. He had taken on large debts to British firms owed by his wife's father at the time of his death.

Much of it was interest that had piled up as the debts went unpaid for many years. Sometimes he sold slaves to meet such obligations, but he tried to keep slave families together and to protect the elderly. He disliked selling slaves so much that he did his best to keep his name out of the papers in connection with such sales.

Looking to his farms, Jefferson found that in his ten years away from home they had been cared for badly. He set out to restore their fertility by an elaborate system of crop rotation. He preferred growing wheat to tobacco because the grain supplied food and needed less labor. But much of the harvest was consumed by his slaves. To increase production he reorganized the work system and introduced labor-saving devices. This is when he improved the moldboard plow he had sketched in France. He also had a portable horse-powered threshing machine built on an English design and soon began harvesting with it.

With all the improvements, he still did not raise enough to support his establishment. To enlarge his income he set up a small factory, worked by a dozen young slaves ten to sixteen years old under a military form of discipline. They got out a ton of nails per month, and for a while the sales met all Jefferson's hopes. Then cheaper nails imported from England ruined his market. Added to his nailery was another home industry, a weaving house. With as many as thirty-five spindles operated by female slaves he had trained, he was able to meet the clothing needs of his large labor force.

How did Jefferson treat his slaves?

The evidence can be gathered from the careful records he kept of the daily life and labor on his farms. A painstaking study recently made of these documents by Professor Jack McLaughlin reveals much that has been passed over in earlier biographies. Jefferson, he wrote, "most certainly realized the debt he owed to slaves—that the civilized elegance of Monticello was made possible by an institution he publicly condemned."

A lyrical view of Monticello, when Jefferson was surrounded by his daughters and their families

Undeniably Jefferson was more humane in the treatment of his slaves than most slaveholders, but he could also order the flogging of slaves. McLaughlin speculates that a man who kept his emotions under tight control could explode in terrible violence. As we have seen, Jefferson bought and sold slaves when his financial needs dictated, and he hired slaves from other masters and put his own slaves out for hire. He treated black people like so many commodities to be traded in the market. Yet, like many slaveholders, he could not blind himself to what he was doing. It made the Virginia gentlemen uncomfortable enough to avoid uttering the word "slave." Instead, they liked to refer to them as "my people" or "my servants."

How those "servants" felt about their condition is implicit in Jefferson's records. The boys who worked in his nail shop, for instance, were always a headache to him. Teenagers full of the juices of life, they were confined to a manufacturing operation for twelve hours a day, six days a week. The work was repetitive, boring, mindless. It offered no room for imagination or inventiveness. And rebelling against dehumanizing tasks, they did as little work as possible. Only when they were closely watched were the young slaves productive. If the overseer or Jefferson himself was not there, little or no work got done.

With Jefferson absent for a long period, one overseer relied on the whip to get work out of the boys. As soon as Jefferson heard this, he made the man quit that degrading punishment. Instead, for a task well done, he offered the slaves rewards: cash, food, clothing. To a couple of adult slaves who sometimes supervised the nailery, he even gave a small share of the profits. Yet these gestures did not end the "idleness" and "mischief" he complained of.

Several of the young slaves in his sweatshop ran away to freedom, and some were hunted down relentlessly. One slave, Jamey Hubbard, ran away once, was brought back, ran away again, was caught and severely flogged in front of the

Jefferson's slave, Isaac, in a daguerreotype of 1845, made nearly twenty years after Jefferson's death. Isaac left a memoir of life at Monticello as seen from the slave's viewpoint.

1822	Wormly	Jerry	Isaac	Ned	Total	
Aug 6	24	22	23	23	92	
7	- -	- - -	8	7	15	
8	16	20	17	13	66	
9 10	- -	- -	- -	34	34	
12	- -	- -	- -	18	18	
13	- -	- -	- -	24	24	
14	13	19	17	7	56	305
15	21	21	10	26	78	
16	20	15	28	26	89	
17	20	20	20	21	81	
19	19	20	20	20	80	328
20	- -	- - -	17	18	35	
21	11	11	18	19	59	
22	20	8	22	21	71	
23	20	11	20	19	70	
24	18	18	19	19	74	309
26	16	19	- - -	14	49	
27	19	9	20	18	66	
28	20	20	20	21	81	
29	15	15	15	15	60	256
						1198

In this page from Jefferson's record of slave labor, dated 1822, the middle column shows Isaac's daily productivity in hauling stone. The stone was probably used in the construction of steps and floors at Monticello.

other slaves, but fled a third time. Jefferson then sold him cheaply, for a rebellious slave brought a low price.

Another slave, Billy, stabbed an overseer, escaped from jail, and joined a band of runaway slaves living off the land. Captured, he was sentenced to be branded on the hand and whipped. Four other young slaves who attacked an overseer were sent by Jefferson to New Orleans to be auctioned off. No matter how paternalistic a master might be, many African-Americans hated their enslavement and resisted it as best they could.

When one of Jefferson's slave blacksmiths, Joe Fosset, ran away to visit Edy, a slave he loved, Jefferson couldn't understand it. Here was a man who had always obeyed orders, never been beaten, and seemed happy. "A runaway like Joe Fosset," writes McLaughlin, "represented a threat to the slave system, for if a slave who was well treated, trained to a trade, and seemingly content ran away, then the institution itself was suspect."

No wonder slaveholders were always sniffing out insurrection. One means of avoiding that terrifying possibility was to keep slaves from communicating with one another. How? By denying them the chance to learn to read and write. Slave artisans, however, were more valuable if they were literate, so skilled white workers in Jefferson's employ probably taught their black apprentices to read or write. Jefferson himself seems to have taught none of them, although he recognized how helpful it was to him if they could read the print in the handbooks for artisans. But writing? No, for they could use that skill to forge documents to help them escape.

Of course the field hands—men and women—were taught no skills: only their muscle was needed for manual farm labor. We know much less about them than about the slave artisans and house slaves. They are only names on his records, with birth dates or their purchase or sale recorded. He moved them about his various farms as needed.

Jefferson seems to have shown greater concern for how his slaves were fed and clothed and doctored than the usual planter. Since anyone in that time could practice medicine (no license was needed), Jefferson trusted more to his own knowledge than to any doctor's. When at Monticello, he cared for the slaves' health himself. He brought Jenner's vaccine from Boston to vaccinate all his slaves against the terrible smallpox scourge. He set broken bones, lanced abscesses, and sewed up wounds. He often reminded his overseers to distribute clothing, keep the slave cabins in repair, and provide enough food.

The slave cabins were usually one-room log homes, perhaps with loft, fireplace and chimney, table, benches or chairs, and a bed. His house slaves ate off imported porcelain dinnerware thrown out by the master when they were chipped or broken. Some of the slaves ate and slept in the buildings where they worked. When the two dependency wings of Monticello were finished during his presidency, the house slaves moved into these superior rooms.

Monticello was no Garden of Eden in these years of retirement. Bad weather eroded the fields, olive and orange trees brought from Italy did not take, nor did sugar maples from New England. Even family life turned sour. Martha's husband, Randolph, half a year after Jefferson's return, grew strangely sick and journeyed north in search of doctors who might cure him. Long considered somewhat odd by friends, he seems to have suffered a mental breakdown. Perhaps living in the shadow of a genius like Jefferson only made it worse. By mid-1795 Jefferson thought Randolph's condition "nearly hopeless," and took his two grandchildren, now four and two, to live with him while their parents went to live on their own plantation.

Jefferson himself was not doing well. He wrote Madison in April 1795 that "my health is entirely broken down within the last eight months." He had been attacked by rheumatism, a catchall term then for what could be strained muscles, arthritis, or several other things. It might have been an injury from lifting something heavy while teaching slaves how to plow. The painful disability plagued him for many years. By broken-down health he may also have meant what only became clear seven years later when he warned his daughter Maria that she must not withdraw from society, as he feared she was doing. "I can speak from experience on this subject. From 1793 to 1797 I remained closely at home, saw none but those who came there, and at length became very sensible of the ill effect it had upon my own mind. . . . It led to an antisocial and misanthropic state of mind, which severely punishes him who gives in to it, and it will be a lesson I never shall forget as to myself."

In that self-imposed isolation he would not even read the newspapers. He was trying to avoid politics, but some events beyond his control cut into his isolation. In the summer of 1794 farmers in western Pennsylvania rebelled against the collection of a federal tax on whiskey. Hundreds of them joined in armed rebellion and burned the tax collectors' offices. In those mountains grain could not be carried across the high ridges in bushel form, so it was converted to the liquid form of easily transportable whiskey. Used for barter, it was the only source of income for the farmers.

Alexander Hamilton, still the treasury secretary, had imposed a tax so heavy that it took about 50 percent of the farmers' income. And Hamilton insisted it be paid in U.S. currency, which was just what the farmers did not have. At the news of the uprising President Washington furiously denounced "this insurrection." The Federalists cried "treason" and demanded military action. Washington himself rode at the head of 13,000 soldiers toward the embattled farmers. Under the threat of force the farmers went home before the troops reached them.

Jefferson sympathized with the farmers, but spoke his mind only in private conversation or letters to friends. The grand display of federal power against what he called a just protest against an "infernal tax" seemed ridiculous. He believed Hamilton and the Federalists were trying to identify the Republicans with lawlessness and disorder. Worse, Washington, who could not see the need for political opposition, spoke up on Hamilton's side. In his next annual message to Congress the president blamed the farmers' resistance to the law on certain "self-created societies"—meaning the Republican groups, the Jeffersonians.

A year later another important piece of news—the signing of the Jay Treaty—aroused Jefferson's anger. Again he saw it as a "monumental folly" created by Hamilton. The treaty had just been ratified by the Senate after a long and heated debate. It was negotiated by John Jay, chief justice of the Supreme Court, as special envoy to England. The aim was to settle the acute differences with England (discussed earlier) which had moved the two nations to the edge of war. Several of its terms were acceptable, but some issues the Republicans thought important were not touched. The Republicans took the lead in whipping up popular opposition, but lost out.

Jefferson would not contribute publicly to the debate, although he believed this was a Federalist betrayal of America to the British. The Jay Treaty hurt him in the pocketbook too, for one of its provisions made it possible for British merchants to get more money out of Americans, like Jefferson, who thought they had already settled such debts.

When it seemed likely that Washington would not seek a third term, Madison wrote his best friend, Jefferson, that he (Jefferson) would be the obvious Republican candidate to succeed the president. No, said Jefferson, the spice of ambition he had savored in younger days was long since evaporated. Not politics, but architecture, consumed him now.

In the spring of 1796 he began to remodel and enlarge the house at Monticello. It had been only half-finished during the Revolutionary years and, in his long absence afterwards, had gone into "almost total decay." How the mansion looks today is the outcome of the transformation begun in these retirement years.

The beautiful town houses he had seen in Paris gave him fresh ideas, and he liked too the one-story mansions in the French countryside. Their interiors were 16 or 18 feet high in the rooms for entertainment, but the bedroom wings were in two tiers, 8 to 10 feet high, each with a small private staircase. He applied this style at Monticello, doubling the outside dimensions of the house and adding a dome modeled on one he had admired in Paris. While still in office at Philadelphia he had ordered building materials to be assembled. Once at home, he had slaves make the bricks he needed. There was work still to be done after he returned to public service in 1797; the house would not be completed until 1809. Visitors to Monticello thought it "one of the most elegant" private homes in America.

The cost of tearing down much of the old house and rebuilding and expanding it was great. To raise money he mortgaged a very large number of his slaves, believing he would never have to deliver them to his creditors. It illustrates a truth about what is probably the most extraordinary building in America: that it was made possible only by a system of slavery that ruthlessly exploited a people brought here against their will.

In September 1796 Washington gave the country his farewell address. It launched the Federalists and the Republicans on a fierce fight for the highest office. (The Republican party of Jefferson's time was not the same as the Republican party of Lincoln and the present, but actually the forerunner of what is now the Democratic party.) It was the first time political parties contested for the presidency. Jefferson knew of course that the Republicans were pushing him to succeed Washington. He didn't ask them to stop, but neither did he promote his own candidacy. Vice President John Adams, the Federalist candidate, thought it unseemly to campaign and sat back waiting. The two men had once been close comrades in the struggle for American independence, but clashing political views had strained the friendship.

During the heated campaign Republicans accused Federalists of trying to erect a constitutional monarchy like Great Britain's. Federalists accused Republicans of trying to foster a radical democracy. Each claimed the other wanted to overthrow the Republic. When the electoral votes were counted, Adams had 71 and was declared president; Jefferson had 68, and according to the practice then specified by the Constitution, the candidate with the second-highest vote became vice president. So narrow a margin of victory was a sign that Adams's party was growing weaker and Jefferson's stronger.

Jefferson said he never doubted that Adams would win. He was glad to escape the presidency because he was sure no man would ever leave that office with the reputation he carried into it. "I have no ambition to govern men," he said. He predicted that troublesome foreign affairs would create a storm that might shipwreck the party in power. "This is certainly not a moment to covet the helm," he concluded.

In Jefferson's view, Adams was not a dangerous man like Hamilton, and might move away from the politics of that detested enemy. In turn, Adams said he was not worried about working with Jefferson and expected they would get along. In March 1797 the two men were inaugurated at ceremonies in Philadelphia.

A week later, Jefferson took the chair as the newly elected president of the American Philosophical Society, based in Philadelphia. His scientific paper analyzing the remains of a prehistoric animal found in Virginia was read to the members. It was a happy moment for him; he would not know many more in the four turbulent years ahead.

★ 15 ★

VICE PRESIDENT: IN OPPOSITION

The duties of the vice president are limited by the Constitution. There are only two: to preside over the Senate's meetings and to succeed the president if he dies, resigns, or is removed. Jefferson knew that Washington had given Adams little to do, asking his opinion only now and then. That set a precedent. At once Adams made it plain that he would treat Jefferson in much the same way. It seemed inevitable especially when the two men headed parties with conflicting views on almost everything. Still, to be made almost an outsider was a frustrating role for so active a man.

Ten days after the inauguration, Congress recessed and Jefferson returned to Monticello. As a salaried official ($5,000 a year) he could count on a regular income to bolster his shaky finances. Home only six weeks, he was recalled for a special session of Congress. When his friend Madison decided not to stand for reelection to Congress, Jefferson was thrust into party leadership. He had not asked for it, but he would show great skill in politicking from now until he left the White House twelve years later.

President John Adams in 1798, painted by William Winstanley. Jefferson was his vice president and led the Republicans opposing Adams's Federalist policies.

The country faced an immediate crisis with France when Adams took office. The French government was angered by the Jay Treaty with England. It began seizing American ships in French harbors and ordered the American minister to leave France. Adams warned the French that the Americans were "not a degraded people, humiliated under a colonial spirit of fear." But wanting to maintain peace, he sent a three-man commission to Paris to negotiate a settlement.

Feelings against the French mounted so high that anyone who criticized the Adams regime and seemed to favor the French was quickly tarred by the Federalists as un-American. It makes frank discussion of policy issues difficult when your patriotism is questioned. Jefferson himself came under heavy attack when a private letter he had written to his Italian friend Philip Mazzei a year earlier was quoted in the press abroad and at home. Because it was critical of Federalist actions, Jefferson was charged with treasonable opinions. His language was very strong, and some mistakenly took his harsh words to refer to Washington. The newspaper attack was prolonged and painful, but Jefferson decided on a policy of silence. He neither admitted nor denied writing the letter.

As presiding officer of the Senate, Jefferson could see that workable rules needed to be established to govern debate in a civil manner. With time on his hands, he decided to prepare a manual on parliamentary procedure. He had learned much about it during his years in the Virginia legislature, and now he collected material from other sources and especially from the experience of the British Parliament. He applied what he was learning while chairing the Senate during his four years in office and began drafting a manual. Just before his term as vice president ended, he finished work on the *Manual* and had it printed. It was adopted by the Senate at once, and much later, in 1837, by the House as well. His *Manual* is still the core of procedure in the Congress and in the states, with many amendments added since his day.

As relations with France ran downhill, Jefferson hoped that his government would do its best to avoid war. He put peace as the first object of the nation: "I am not for linking ourselves by new treaties with the quarrels of Europe; entering their field of slaughter to preserve their balance, or joining in the confederacy of kings to war against the principles of liberty."

When the Senate closed shop as the summer of 1797 began, he went back to Monticello. The high point of a long stay of five months was the marriage of his daughter Maria to her cousin John Wayles Eppes, a young man Jefferson had fostered almost from infancy and Maria's childhood playmate. The lord of Monticello had the roof of his home removed for new construction and the family had to make do elsewhere while the work continued. In December, leaving the house empty, he returned to Philadelphia for the next session of Congress.

France again roiled the political waters through the so-called XYZ affair. The commissioners Adams had sent to Paris were told by the French foreign minister, Talleyrand, that success of negotiations depended on a prior loan to the French government and a $240,000 bribe to him. When Adams reported this to Congress the Americans were furious. The Federalists denounced the XYZ affair as an insult to American honor and cried out, "Millions for defense, but not one cent for tribute!"

With anti-French feeling running so high, the president denounced "enemies" both at home and abroad for putting the country in the greatest danger. Adams talked of domestic "traitors" seeking to aid an "invading enemy" even though his Republican opponents too had deplored France's behavior. The Jeffersonians watched in alarm as the Federalists took several steps to enlarge the army and navy to repel any French attack and repealed the Franco-American treaty of 1778. With France fighting desperately against other nations in Europe the Jeffersonians didn't believe there was any danger of invasion. They wondered rather if the military was being expanded for use against themselves.

Talk of a conspiracy against the United States, supposedly directed by foreign agents, mounted high. In the summer of 1798 the Federalist-dominated Congress passed four severely restrictive laws. Three were aimed at foreigners—especially Frenchmen and Irishmen—viewed as dangerous revolutionaries. Such aliens could be deported or confined during war. Hundreds of Frenchmen, suspected of being plotters, were thrown out of the country. The fourth and worst law, the Sedition Act, was aimed directly at the Jeffersonian opposition. It made it a crime punishable by fine and imprisonment to speak, write, or publish false, scandalous, and malicious statements about the president, Congress, or the government "with intent to defame" or with intent to "excite against the government the hatred of the people."

The bold moves of the Federalists stunned the Jeffersonians. The laws could smother all political opposition. It was an open declaration of war on Jefferson's followers. The Federalists were saying that the policies of those in power were above criticism.

To carry out the Alien Acts the Administration began an elaborate system of investigations meant to force all foreigners to register. Large numbers of aliens decided to leave the country. Several prosecutions were begun, but the people targeted went into hiding before they could be picked up. Even more people were prosecuted under the Sedition Act. At least twenty-five were arrested and charged with violating the act. Fifteen were indicted and ten were convicted, most of them Jeffersonian printers and editors.

Among those persecuted for their political opinions—to give but one example—was David Brown, a veteran of the Revolutionary War and a merchant seaman. Settling in Dedham, Massachusetts, in 1789, he began to write political pamphlets attacking leaders of the government for grab-

A cartoonist depicts the sensational fight on the floor of Congress in 1798 between Republican Matthew Lyon of Vermont and Federalist Roger Griswold of Connecticut. Lyon was indicted under the Sedition Act for criticizing President John Adams. He was reelected to Congress while in jail.

bing the western lands for themselves. From what he had read and observed he was certain that government was the tool of the rich to exploit the poor. His radical words brought about his arrest on charges of defaming the government and aiding its enemies. Lacking bail, he was thrown into prison. Tried in 1799 before a Federalist judge determined to make him an example, Brown was declared guilty. The court demanded he name his accomplices and provide a list of the people who had brought his pamphlets. He refused, protesting that he would "lose all my friends." He was sentenced to a fine of $480 and eighteen months in jail. Unable to pay his fine, he could have stayed behind bars indefinitely, for people could be jailed for debt in those days. (Some two years later, when Jefferson became president, he was freed.)

This was the first manifestation of a fear of the outsider, the alien, the dissenter, all jumbled together in the popular mind. Unhappily, the Alien and Sedition period would not be the only time the criminal law would be stretched to cover political dissent. It was but the first. From the early post-Revolutionary time down to today, legislatures have continually tried to curb political movements they disapprove of. Almost any time a citizen protests what some politician or government does he or she is liable to be called "subversive" and made a target for persecution.

News of the Alien and Sedition Acts generated a firestorm of protest. Jefferson thought the Sedition Act was intended to wreck the Republican press and the alien laws to squelch such close allies of his as the Swiss-born Albert Gallatin, leader of the Republicans in Congress. Again home in Monticello, where he spent the last half of 1798, Jefferson rejoiced that meetings to protest the laws were being held throughout Virginia. As for himself, he kept his feelings under cover. He knew any oppositional move he might make would be suspect, even called treasonable. Besides, he thought the delirium induced by the Federalists would in time pass, for the people were basically in sound health.

While Jefferson himself was attacked in the Federalists press, he kept silent. Before he could answer one libel, he said, "twenty new ones would be invented." The public must judge him on his deeds. He made his protests in private to friends. What people think, he said, is not subject to the coercion of the laws. Governmental power extends "to such acts only as are injurious to others." Freedom of thought is an absolute, he believed; "reason and free inquiry are the only effectual agents against error."

Casting about for a weapon against the Alien and Sedition Acts, he turned to the states. Behind the scenes he and James Madison drafted the famous Kentucky and Virginia Resolutions of 1798. The Kentucky assembly passed resolutions drawn up by Jefferson, and then the Virginia assembly adopted others drafted by Madison. The resolutions declared that the national government had violated the Bill of Rights, and that when the central authority threatened the people's liberties, the states "have the right and are in duty bound to interpose for arresting the progress of the evil." This amounted to saying that the states had the right to set aside a federal law they considered unconstitutional. Only a handful of people knew the men who had written these precedent-setting resolutions. Taking this rash step, Jefferson went beyond most of his party. He adopted an extreme states' rights position.

Little support for the resolutions was voiced anywhere else. Nor did either Kentucky or Virginia attempt to obstruct the federal laws. Still, the resolutions had an effect in demonstrating how deep was the opposition to the Federalist program. Over the long term, however, Jefferson's Kentucky Resolutions had another effect, and a poisonous one. They claimed the power of the states to nullify acts of Congress. And as North and South split over the slavery issue in the decades ahead, the threat of nullification—and ultimately secession—became a powerful weapon in the hands of the proslavery forces.

There is another important aspect to Jefferson's resolutions. They reveal that contrary to the Jefferson myth, he was not really an advocate of absolute freedom of the press. In his Kentucky draft he was saying that the Sedition Act was void not because a free, republican government could not punish the press for verbal crimes, but rather because the power to punish such crimes belonged "solely and exclusively" to the states, *not* the federal government. So to Jefferson the press *could* be controlled—but only by the states. Later, as president, he would urge a state to prosecute a Federalist newspaper for what he called seditious libel.

It is curious to see what little time the duties of government required top officials to spend in their offices during the early years of the Republic. In his four-year term as vice president, Jefferson's calendar shows that he spent a total of twenty-one months at the capital in Philadelphia and twenty-seven months at Monticello. There he lived in almost complete isolation from the world outside. His community consisted of his immediate family and about a hundred slaves. This was the tranquil life he said he loved. But one wonders whether it was solely a sense of civic duty that always had him returning to the hurly-burly of the political arena.

He found great pleasure in his work with the American Philosophical Society. In 1799 (the third year of his presidency of the APS) he had a circular issued to encourage the pursuit of research in the natural sciences, archeology, and ethnology. He laid special emphasis on the study of the "customs, manners, languages and character of the Indian nations, ancient and modern, and their migrations." To that end he called for research on Indian mounds, and the recovery of artifacts from them. He also pressed for new evidence of the remains of unknown and extinct animals, such as the mammoth. Robert Livingston's encouragement of the use of steamboat fascinated him, and he wrote the financier suggesting exploration of other applications for the use of steam power.

While recognizing that scientific systems should be built on facts, in his own thinking Jefferson sometimes ventured into fantasy. Nothing wrong in that, for knowledge often profits from a scientist's speculation or guesswork. And Jefferson was open-minded, willing to admit error in himself. The noted French scientist of his day, Georges Cuvier, praised Jefferson for "an enlightened love and extensive knowledge of the sciences" to which he had contributed much. Harlow Shapley, the distinguished Harvard astronomer of our own time, wrote that, "Like all daring thinkers and workers in the pioneer days of so many of the sciences, Jefferson went off the deep end a few times." He pointed out that these failures were few as compared with his successes. "He had, as they say, pretty nearly everything. In the field of natural philosophy he had caution and daring, inquisitiveness and a willingness to change his mind in the light of new facts or as a result of further thought. What we would now call proper scientific methods appeared to be instinctive with him."

It was during his vice presidency that Jefferson tried to lay the basis for his long-cherished goal of founding a new state university in Virginia. He thought little of his own College of William and Mary, still tied to the Anglican church. He hoped to start a new university in the healthier climate of upper Virginia. Its program would be liberal and modern, stressing the sciences and appealing to students nationwide. He shared his ideas with the noted English scientist Dr. Joseph Priestley, the discoverer of oxygen. Persecuted at home for his radical views, Priestley had migrated to Pennsylvania. He responded to Jefferson with suggestions for a science curriculum.

For the last ten months of 1799 Jefferson was at Monticello, trying to make his still incomplete house livable. He had a roof placed over the north end and got the floors laid in its many rooms. The families of both his daughters were now with him. He prepared an appendix for an edition of his *Notes on Virginia* to be published in 1800.

IDEAS AND INVENTIONS

In Jefferson's study of Native American cultures, he collected this carved stone statuette of a "pregnant woman kneeling."

This clock, made to Jefferson's specifications, was mounted over the entrance hall of Monticello.

The jawbone of a mastodon owned by Jefferson and displayed at Monticello in his later years

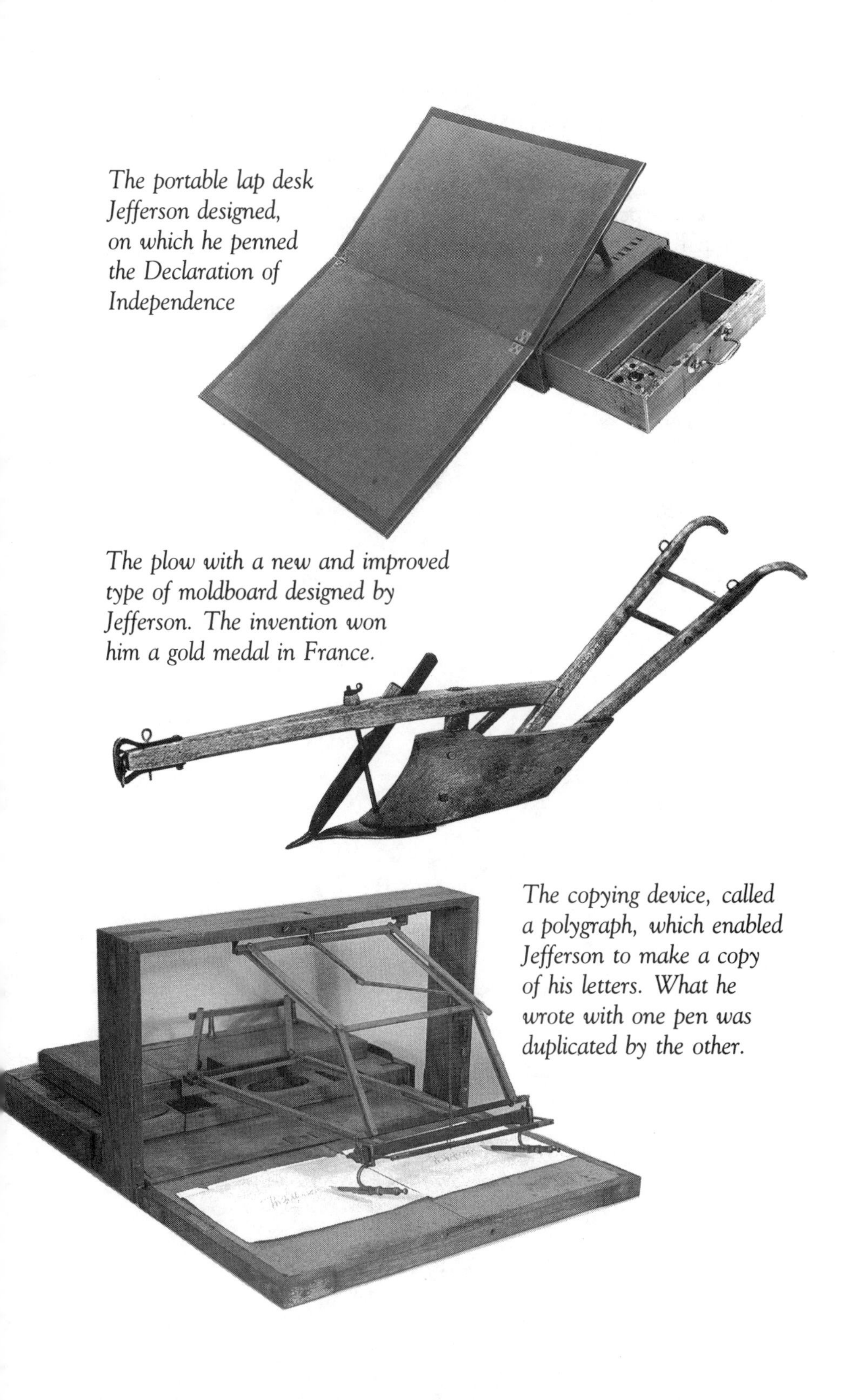

The portable lap desk Jefferson designed, on which he penned the Declaration of Independence

The plow with a new and improved type of moldboard designed by Jefferson. The invention won him a gold medal in France.

The copying device, called a polygraph, which enabled Jefferson to make a copy of his letters. What he wrote with one pen was duplicated by the other.

President Adams had left Philadelphia for his home in Massachusetts. He was attacked by some Federalists for renewing negotiations with France. But, said Adams, "the end of war is peace, and peace is offered to me." He had decided that his only hope of reelection was to create a peace coalition out of both parties. By the year's end the American commissioners to Paris had secured an agreement to restore peaceful relations between the two powers.

★ 16 ★

WINNING THE PRESIDENCY

By the year 1800 the United States had solidly established the world's first democratic republic. Its territory covered 880,000 square miles. Its population—five million—had doubled in size since the founding. Many of the people had become prosperous, with a greater proportion of them owning land than the Europeans did, and more had a say in government policy.

But it was a democracy for whites only. Almost one-fifth of the population—900,000—were slaves, and eight of the sixteen states sanctioned slavery. America was now the largest slaveholding country in the world.

The country was—and would remain so for a long time—overwhelmingly rural. Of every twenty people, nineteen lived on farms or in villages. The biggest cities were Philadelphia, with 70,000 people, and New York, with 60,000. Then came the smaller cities: Baltimore, 26,000; Boston, 25,000; Charleston, 20,000. Only seven other cities could claim more than 5,000.

The cities were controlled by small groups: merchants, traders, lawyers, and "gentlemen" at the top, with tradesmen, shopkeepers, and master craftsmen and their journeymen below. All the other city folk—three-fourths of the population—had nothing to say about how they were ruled. This large majority were the unskilled workers, apprentices, sailors, servants, slaves, and rabble. But it was not a rigid society. Anyone who could climb up the commercial ladder into the wealthy class was admitted to power.

The year 1800 was an election year. It found the Federalists divided. The political profit they had made from the troubles with France was now spent. With peace a reality, they faced a public angry over the unconstitutional use of federal power and the gagging of political dissent. The Hamiltonian wing of the Federalists was disgusted with John Adams and wanted him to quit office at the end of his term. When he refused to withdraw, they plotted his defeat.

Such disunity made it easier, of course, for the Republicans. To head their ticket a large caucus agreed unanimously to support Jefferson for president and Aaron Burr for vice president. Jefferson distrusted the New Yorker but accepted him for his political usefulness. Working quietly with small groups, Republican leaders welded together a powerful party. They financed newspapers, printed and circulated pamphlets, organized congressmen to get out the vote in their districts.

With the congressional session ended—it was the last time the government would meet in Philadelphia—Jefferson left for home late in May.

While looking to his house and his plantations he kept in touch with political developments through correspondence. He did no public campaigning, leaving that to friends and the party press. The press was even more violent in its charges and countercharges than in 1796. Federalist editors called the Jeffersonians "poison-sucking toads" and Republicans returned the abuse in kind. Both sides acted as though the survival of the nation was at stake. His biographer Dumas Malone believes the charges hurled at Jefferson were "more

A Federalist cartoon of the 1800 election campaign. It depicts the American eagle preventing Jefferson from destroying the Constitution on an "Altar to Gallic Despotism," as the eye of Heaven looks on.

reckless than those against Adams and much less relevant. Indeed, it may be claimed that the personal attacks on the chief Republican were the most vicious in any presidential campaign on record. One may doubt if a more distorted picture of a candidate for the first office has ever been presented by his foes."

It was the clergy's repeated attacks upon Jefferson, calling him an atheist, an infidel, a fanatic, even a man guilty of fraud and robbery, that brought from him one of his most cherished utterances. He thought his personal religious beliefs were nobody's business but his own. But in a private letter to his friend Dr. Benjamin Rush, discussing the issue,

Jefferson placed his initials in the center of his wax seal. He put above them his words, "Rebellion to Tyrants Is Obedience to God."

he said, "I have sworn upon the altar of God eternal hostility against any form of tyranny over the mind of man." The pamphlets that lied about him are forgotten, but these words light up the wall of the Jefferson Memorial in Washington.

In November Jefferson left Monticello for Washington, where the government had moved in June. He roomed in a boarding house close by what there was of the Capitol, for half of it was still not built. From his windows he could see the infant city changing rapidly. Groves of trees were being cut down to make room for new construction or for use as firewood. "The unnecessary felling of a tree," he wrote, "perhaps the growth of centuries, seems to me a crime little short of murder; it pains me to an unspeakable degree."

By mid-December the decisive victory of Jefferson and Burr over Adams was confirmed in the state vote for electors. But a tie occurred in the Electoral College, with each man getting 73 votes. Which would be president, Jefferson or Burr? Because of the tie the final decision, under the Constitution, was thrown into the Federalist House of Representatives, elected two years earlier, where a deadlock quickly occurred. Although pressured by Jefferson's supporters, Burr refused to

Aaron Burr, vice president during Jefferson's first administration

give way. The Federalist caucus decided to back Burr, thinking him the lesser evil. But Hamilton thought anyone would make a better president than Burr—even Jefferson. He helped swing enough votes to Jefferson to elect him on the thirty-sixth ballot. That the Federalists had lost their grip on the country was proved in the congressional elections, for the Republicans won majorities in both House and Senate.

The election marked the end of Federalist power, and the rise of the Republicans. It should be noted that theirs was the party of slavery. Jefferson had won over 85 percent of the vote cast by states in which slavery was the fundamental fact of social and economic life. Although Jefferson was torn by the conflict between his frequent declaration of belief in human liberty and his ownership of slaves, his attitude was not shared by most of those who voted for him. They, like Jefferson, were frightened by the news of recent slave rebellions. The blacks of Haiti had risen against their masters, killed the whites unable to flee, and under Toussaint L'Ouverture's leadership had created a free black republic.

In the summer of 1800, while Jefferson was at Monticello, thousands of Virginia slaves were reported to have joined a plot conceived by Gabriel, a free black, to attack Richmond, kill whites, and then escape to Indian country in the West. When an informer aborted the conspiracy, hundreds of slaves were rounded up and over thirty were given a summary trial and executed. Hearing the terrible news, Jefferson said, "We [meaning the whites] are truly to be pitied!"

As white hysteria threatened to take the lives of many more blacks, Jefferson warned that such revenge would turn public opinion at home and abroad against Virginia. (Besides, no white persons had been harmed by any of the alleged conspirators.) He urged Governor Monroe to deport rather than execute the accused slaves. But no one was willing to take them, and most of Gabriel's followers were sold as slaves in Spanish or Portuguese colonies.

To take office as president, Jefferson had to wait until March 4, the date for beginning a new administration. Meanwhile the Federalist lame duck Congress passed a Judiciary Act entrenching their party's control of at least this one branch of government.

The bitterly divisive years seemed over. No one knew what would come next. How capable a national leader would Jefferson be? What kind of America would he shape at the beginning of this new century?

Just before noon on March 4, 1801, Jefferson left his boarding house and walked to the Senate chamber in the Capitol to be inaugurated as the third president of the Republic. In silent reaction to Federalist pomp and ceremony, he was dressed plainly and accompanied not by a cavalcade but only by some friends. The retiring president, John Adams, with whom he was no longer speaking, had left Washington hours before. After the oath of office was given by the new chief justice, John Marshall, Jefferson began his inaugural address. His weak voice reached only the first rows of the crowded chamber. The others had to read it the next day in the Washington papers. His manner was informal and friendly, and his words carried a healing message. "We are all republicans; we are all federalists," he said, calling on everyone "to unite in common efforts for the common good." Then, assuring his opponents that he would respect the rights of a minority: "If there be any among us who would wish to dissolve this Union or to change its republican form, let them stand undisturbed as monuments of the safety with which error of opinion may be tolerated where reason is left free to combat it."

The speech was magnificent, a classic statement of both political and personal philosophy: "A good government," he said, is "a wise and frugal government, which shall restrain men from injuring one another, which shall leave them otherwise free to regulate their own pursuits of industry and im-

The incomplete Capitol in Washington during Jefferson's presidency

provement, and shall not take from the mouth of labor the bread it has earned."

Did he mean these words to be universally applied? He could not have forgotten his own slaves when he spoke of not taking "from the mouth of labor the bread it has earned." Or, as some have argued, did he mean that though this was not the case now, it *would* be someday?

And again, referring to the bitter friction between the contending political parties, he said, "Let us restore to social intercourse, that harmony and affection without which liberty and even life itself are but dreary things."

He had taken only two weeks to prepare his inaugural address, using no secretary and consulting no sources. He needed no speech-writer to put ideas into his head or words into his mouth. The country was deeply impressed with the memorable speech, and happy that the switch from the first governing party to a rival one had taken place peacefully. He assured Americans, "though the will of the majority is in all cases to prevail, that will, to be rightful, must be reasonable, that the minority possess their equal rights, which equal laws must protect, and to violate would be oppression."

So he had set out for the nation a testament of his beliefs and a promise to maintain freedom and equality of opportunity. This great new experiment in government was the center of the world's attention. Nothing like it could be seen anywhere else, for the French Revolution had turned into one-man rule by General Napoleon Bonaparte. The new president's goal was to extend democracy even further, and to make it work well.

★ 17 ★

WHAT POWER CAN DO

At last Jefferson was at the peak of national power. He had held several high governmental posts before, but in none could he exercise his own will this freely. His first task was to assemble a loyal crew to help him steer the ship of state. The government was tiny as compared with now. Only some 300 federal employees could be appointed or removed by the president. Below them were about 700 clerks chosen by their superiors. Most of the remaining 3,000 civilian employees worked for the postal system.

Jefferson wanted no wholesale purge of Federalists. He would fire only the corrupt or incompetent, and maybe some stubborn Hamiltonians. He didn't intend to introduce what later would be called the spoils system—that is, the ousting of all jobholders who did not belong to the party that won the election and their replacement by the faithful. Merit, not influence, would be his guiding line.

But he faced some complications. When President Adams learned he had lost to Jefferson, he had filled every vacancy in government with diehard Federalists. His most important appointment was John Marshall as chief justice of the

The Jefferson portrait, painted by Rembrandt Peale in 1800, now hangs in the White House. It is considered one of the most popular images of the president.

Supreme Court. Under the new judiciary law created by the last Federalist Congress, Adams had also appointed a great number of judges, marshals, and attorneys just before he left office.

The other big problem was that Jefferson's own supporters wanted him to fire all the Federalists to make room for good Republicans. Under heavy pressure from his own party Jefferson began to modify his merit principle. He decided he would have to reward the faithful, appointing people on political grounds so long as they were also competent. He gave in to pressure enough to create a federal job turnover of about 50 percent during his first term. His appointees were mostly from the educated gentry; at least he was raising the quality of officeholders, he thought.

When it came to the crucial cabinet posts, he chose only dedicated Republicans who shared his views. They would run the Departments of War and the Navy and the Attorney General's Office. To head the key positions of state and treasury, however, he wanted brilliance as well as loyalty, and made James Madison and Albert Gallatin his closest associates. Madison had an intensely personal relationship with Jefferson, almost son to father, and they balanced one another well in desirable talents. Gallatin's link to him was less personal and more intellectual. He knew more about public finances than either Jefferson or Madison and could figure out for them how to do what they desired.

Jefferson handled his cabinet superbly, maintaining a calm, cooperative atmosphere with plenty of room for differences of opinion. But in the end, discussion nearly always reached unanimous decision. His door was always open to them as individuals, and they were often his dinner guests as well. Easygoing though he was, his stature as leader was so commanding that no one could forget who was in charge.

The same tactful managerial skill was shown in the way Jefferson worked with the Congress. Neither Washington nor Adams had done as well, and few presidents who followed

James Madison, a close friend of Jefferson, and chosen as his secretary of state

Jefferson could match his finesse. A political analyst of his administration, Forrest McDonald, wrote that "He used none of the techniques that are usually associated with 'strong' presidents—popular pressure, naked power, bribery, flattery, cajolery, blackmail, or shrewd trading—yet he had but to suggest legislation and it was almost invariably forthcoming."

How did he do it? By the personal way he dealt with the legislators. He reached out to them one by one, or in small groups, inviting carefully chosen members of both parties to his dinner table. There, as McDonald describes it, "Always unwigged, sometimes dressed in frayed homespun and rundown slippers, the president put his guests at their ease with the folksy, open hospitality of a country squire; but the dinner (prepared by a French chef and accompanied by a magnificent selection of French wines) was likely to be the finest the legislators had ever tasted, and the conversation was regularly the most fascinating they ever heard. Jefferson always led the conversation, dazzling his guests by talking with equal ease of architecture, history, science, theology, music, mathematics, or art—everything but current politics, which subject was forbidden."

The effect was usually to capture their support. They returned to the business of the House and Senate enormously impressed by the wisdom and virtue of the president. There was more behind his success, of course. Gallatin became his major link with the Congress, helping the Republicans to shape bills the president desired and working with party caucuses to organize the vote for them. His cabinet members also drafted bills for Congress, giving its committees information and testifying before them. Thus the executive branch was able to wield great influence on the legislative process. At that time the Congress itself had no staff, nor did its members. They did not even have offices—only their desk in the legislative chamber. (Today, standing behind every single member of Congress is a strong staff. The House has about 11,000 aides, and the Senate 7,000.)

The president himself worked very hard at his job, rising at 5 A.M., doing his paper work till 9, then meeting with cabinet officers or others with business to look after. Congressmen could drop in any time without an appointment. Cabinet meetings would be held around noon. At 1 P.M. Jefferson took a horseback ride for exercise. Around 3:30 came dinner; he might dine with a personal friend, and about three times a week with many guests, including the legislators. The guests were gone by 6, and he went back to his writing desk. He did paperwork till 10, when he usually went to bed. His work schedule consumed ten or twelve hours a day, leaving him only some four hours "for riding, dining and a little unbending," he said.

During the regular two-month summer recess of Congress he moved his presidential office to Monticello. If important issues were pending he kept one cabinet officer in

Washington, arranging for special couriers to get mail to him in two days. While at home he could consult easily with Madison, his closest adviser, who lived only 30 miles away.

In contrast to some modern presidents who have not wanted to be bothered with detail, he had his cabinet send him every day a packet of the more important letters they received, with their drafts of replies. Running the government was *his* duty, and he meant to be fully responsible for decisions. He wrote all his own letters (copying them on a press), as well as his state papers. He had one private secretary (the first was the young army officer from Virginia, Meriwether Lewis) whom he used mainly as liaison with Congress. His annual message to Congress he circulated in draft form to the cabinet, asking their suggestions for revision. He met with the cabinet not weekly but whenever necessary. Since their offices were nearby the President's House, this was easily done. In his cabinet, unlike Washington's, where he and Hamilton had clashed bitterly, all was smooth and comfortable. His style was to persuade, not dictate. The result: his principal cabinet heads stayed with him throughout his two terms in office.

This aristocrat preferred democratic simplicity to showiness. He ended the ceremonial pomp Washington had introduced and that Adams continued. He gave up formal receptions and quit obeying the formal rules of diplomatic etiquette. It distressed some foreign diplomats. A British minister felt insulted when he showed up in full diplomatic uniform to present his credentials and was met by Jefferson in shabby old clothes and slippers. Nor did he feel any better when at dinner the guests were told to sit anywhere they wished.

Sticking to his habit of keeping meticulous records, Jefferson found that his household and office expenses during his first year in office came to over $16,000. He paid this out of his annual salary of $25,000. At the year's end, he had to borrow $4,000 to balance his personal budget.

Th: Jefferson requests the favour of The Honble Genl. Mattoon to dine with him the day after tomorrow — — at half after three, or at whatever later hour the house may rise.

Monday Feb. 1st 1802.

The favour of an answer is asked.

The form Jefferson used to invite dinner guests to the White House, and a section of the record he kept of his dinner guests

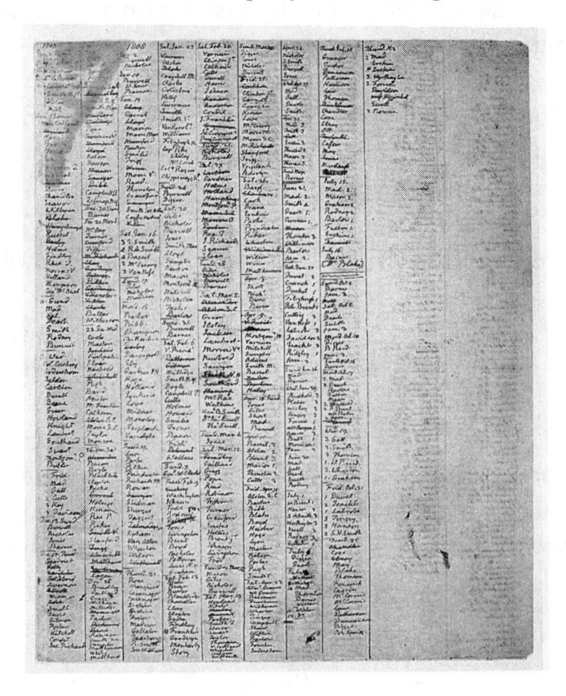

It was during his first term that Jefferson gave several evenings to snipping passages from the Gospels of Matthew, Mark, Luke, and John and pasting them on blank pages to create his version of "The Philosophy of Jesus." He had given much thought to religion after the attacks upon him during the 1800 campaign. Was he irreligious? He tried to define his own belief by close study of the early Christian documents. It convinced him that to the authentic moral teachings of Jesus later writers had added supernatural elements. His forty-six-page compilation removed those, leaving, as he said, "the most sublime and benevolent code of morals which has ever been offered to man." This was but one example of how he found time somehow to pursue his intellectual interests while never neglecting the heavy duties of the presidency.

Shortly after his inauguration, Jefferson moved from the boarding house to the President's House. It was built of sandstone, and painted white. At this time it lacked the north and south porticos, which would not be added till the 1820s. Jefferson had the low arcaded wings built and the leaky roof replaced during his tenure. The huge mansion was still unfinished, but he had become used to such inconvenience at Monticello. To staff the twenty-three-room house he acquired two stewards, about a dozen domestic servants, and a French chef. He had his own riding horse, and bought four others to draw the carriage he ordered made.

In the room that he made his study he kept his books, scientific instruments, paints and palette, maps and globe, a set of carpenter tools and another of gardening tools. On the window ledges he placed potted roses and geraniums. His pet mockingbird, kept here in a cage, often flew freely about the study, perching on his shoulder as he worked or singing atop his table. When he climbed the stairs to his bedroom, the bird would hop up after him. "He could not live without something to love," wrote a woman friend, "and in the absence of his darling grandchildren, his bird and his flowers became the objects of tender care."

His inventiveness found play in this mansion as well as at Monticello. He designed a closet with a circular rack pivoting at the center. When the door was opened, the rack could be turned to show the jackets and breeches hanging from it. He also designed for his study a novel map case. Several maps were rolled on cylinder shafts so that any one could be pulled out, suspended for study, and then released and rolled back on its shaft.

Looking back at his first term, a few events stand out as of great importance. The Federalist-dominated court system presented one major issue. Adams's last-minute judicial appointments had converted the national judiciary into a Federalist stronghold against the victorious Jeffersonians. The Republicans held that trickery had given the Federalists control of this branch of government, while they, the Republicans, had earned control of the other two branches by popular vote.

Early on, the Republican Congress repealed the Judiciary Act of 1801, and then passed the Judiciary Act of 1802, keeping all the reforms of the earlier law that suited their partisan interests. It meant that the judges who held their seats under the Adams law would have to be removed. Yet the Constitution said that judges held their seats for life unless removed by impeachment. Was it constitutional to remove these judges? Who would decide? Did the courts have the power to declare legislative acts unconstitutional? The Founding Fathers understood the idea of judicial review, but they did not mention it in the Constitution. Maybe they thought it was implied for surely a law, if it is to be carried out, must be interpreted by judges and their decisions enforced.

The test came soon in the case known as *Marbury* v. *Madison*. Madison, as the new secretary of state, had refused to deliver the appointment warrants of judges chosen by Adams. One of them, William Marbury, sued for his job, and the case reached the Supreme Court in 1803. The Court

John Marshall, chief justice of the Supreme Court

found in favor of Madison, with Chief Justice Marshall writing the decision. He said the law under which Marbury sued was unconstitutional. In his opinion he laid down the principle of judicial review. His justification of the judicial review of an act of Congress by the Supreme Court has served as a precedent ever since. Now the high court had the power to nullify laws that go beyond the government's limited authority.

Neither Jefferson nor Madison liked Marshall's theory, but they couldn't very well fight it since it was embedded in a decision in their own favor. The results of this opinion have been enormous. Many times the Court has used its power to change the course of American history, sometimes, depending on your point of view, doing considerable harm, and at other times great good.

The Jeffersonians also tried to get rid of several highly partisan Federalist judges. Right after the *Marbury* v. *Madison* decision, the House of Representatives impeached John Pickering, a Federal district judge from New Hampshire. He was tried by the Senate in March of 1804. The grounds were not "high crimes and misdemeanors" as the Constitution requires, but erratic behavior on the bench, especially his Federalist assaults on defendants and juries. Eager to purge such judges, the Jeffersonians asserted impeachment was not a criminal process. It was "nothing more than a declaration by Congress" that an individual holds "dangerous opinions" that, if allowed to go into effect, "will work the destruction of the Union." Now that sounded very much like the repressive language the Federalists had used against Jeffersonians in the sedition trials scarcely five years earlier. But the Senate convicted Pickering on a strictly party vote, and he was removed from his judgeship. Evidence at the trial demonstrated that Pickering was insane and hence guilty of no high crimes or misdemeanors. (The Constitution left no way to get rid of a federal judge for incompetence.)

Flushed with that success, the Jeffersonians reached higher with impeachment proceedings against Samuel Chase, a Supreme Court justice. He was a notorious baiter of Republicans who had infuriated them with the way he tried cases under the Sedition Act. His temper exploded on the bench, he insulted Republican lawyers, and he made partisan political speeches to grand juries. He had even denounced from the bench various democratic reform measures he considered would open the gates of government to the ignorant mob. He struck at the ideas Jefferson had written into the Declaration of Independence, though he himself had signed it in his younger and more radical days.

While Chase's words may have been foolish or undemocratic, perhaps even wicked in some eyes, they were his honest views, and in America he was supposed to have every right to speak or write them. Yet it was Jefferson himself who suggested that Chase's public expression of views the president disliked should be made the target of impeachment proceedings. He wrote a congressman he wanted Chase to be punished, but with the understanding that Jefferson's name would be kept out of it.

The trial of Chase revealed that he had committed no impeachable offense under the Constitution. Conviction required a two-thirds vote by the Senate. Chase was found not guilty on any of the counts, and went back to his seat on the Supreme Court. So a constitutional principle was reaffirmed, even in the case of a judge most Americans probably detested. Had Chase's impeachment succeeded, it would have created a political and constitutional crisis.

What this demonstrates is that when Jefferson was president he was much less the civil libertarian than when he did not hold power. (If this was true of such a celebrated apostle of liberty, it was true also of a number of presidents long after him.) Jefferson, like most of the Founding Fathers, believed that in the public world, power conflicted with liberty. Power was not evil in itself, but it was dangerous. Endlessly it tended to expand itself beyond legitimate boundaries. Power was the concern of those who governed, while liberty was the concern of those governed. That was the reason for adopting a Bill of Rights—to protect the individual citizen from the power of government to invade his liberty. Those who exercised power could not be trusted to safeguard liberty; the people should not rely on a president's self-restraint. No matter how benevolent a president or how libertarian in principle, he must be restrained by law.

The arbitrary way Jefferson himself behaved when the newspapers attacked him and his administration illustrates how he could depart so far from his devotion to freedom of the press. He gave his support to state actions for libel against Federalist editors. (But what is libel? Who defines it? It is a matter of interpretation.)

In 1803 the governor of Pennsylvania wrote him complaining of almost daily attacks on the Republicans, and asked his advice on what to do about it. Jefferson replied that "a few prosecutions of the most prominent offenders would have a wholesome effect in restoring the integrity of the presses. Not a general prosecution, for that would look like persecution; but a selected one." His advice was taken, and in both Pennsylvania and New York state courts tried Federalist editors for seditious libel.

When reading Jefferson we sometimes get the impression that he believed in absolute freedom of the press. But the only absolute freedom he would grant the press was from prior censorship. *After* publication the press could be held responsible for slander, seditious libel, or whatever endangered the public peace. But in the state, not the federal courts. Which means he did believe in state control of the press. In his Second Inaugural Address in 1805, he made public his opinion that libelous publications ought to be prosecuted in the state courts.

By the time he would complete his second term, he admitted that his faith in the press had faded. The newspapers had become "prostituted vehicles of passion," he said, full of "daring and atrocious lies." The American press, however, was not as bad as Jefferson charged. There were several papers, partisan though they were, which were fair and responsible. He forgot that the press reflected American culture and the people he said he trusted.

The major triumph of Jefferson's first term was the purchase of the Louisiana Territory. It climaxed a complex series of events in Europe that affected American interests. But that story need not be told in detail here. It is enough to say that Napoleon Bonaparte had forced the king of Spain to give him Louisiana—the vast territory between the Mississippi River and the crest of the Rockies. And then, because the French general Charles Leclerc failed disastrously to subdue the rebelling blacks of Santo Domingo, Napoleon decided to offer the whole province of Louisiana to the Americans and get on with things in Europe. He had no hope of retaining Louisiana in his war with England that was about to resume, so he let it be known that he was willing to sell to the Americans.

American settlers for some time had been moving across the Mississippi into Spanish Louisiana. It was a migration Jefferson approved. For in his view the Republic needed to grow across the North American continent if it was to avoid the decay of urban concentration. As we've seen, he opposed the Federalist drive to build the nation through commerce and manufacturing. It was on the independent yeoman farmer that a healthy future must be built. But that required rapid territorial expansion. Land made available to yeoman citizens would offer opportunity, draw people out of the cities and the crowded lands of the East, and improve the quality of human life.

This thinking lay behind the president's desire to purchase the Louisiana Territory. Early in 1803 he sent James Monroe to Paris to purchase New Orleans and West Florida. When Monroe arrived, he found the French ready to sell *all* of Louisiana. A deal was made. For $15 million the United States acquired nearly 830,000 square miles.

It was one of the most important events in American history. It not only removed the French from competition, but doubled the size of the American empire and thus greatly improved its prospects. Ironically, the purchase was made by foreign loans, and these would not have been offered if Hamilton had not firmly established the credit of the United States.

It was a lucky combination of European circumstances that made the purchase possible. It was so wildly improbable that no one could have predicted it. But when the opportunity came, Jefferson was ready to take advantage of it. His party ardently supported the decision. Land speculators saw the chance to make fat profits, planters on exhausted tobacco farms welcomed an expanded market for their surplus slaves, and the party regulars anticipated great gains from the popularity of the deal. The Federalists, however, feared that southern slaveholders would now have a much greater territory to dominate.

What authority did Jefferson have to purchase Louisiana? None whatever. In the Constitution there was no provision for adding territory. To do it legally, he would have needed to get the adoption of an amendment to the Constitution. He did not seek to do that. As he once said, there were times when the law must be set aside if the needs of a society required it. But who would judge when such action was needed? Presumably, wise and virtuous men—like himself? He wrote:

> On great occasions every good officer must be ready to risk himself in going beyond the strict line of the law, when the public preservation requires it; his motives will be a justification. . . . A strict observance of the written law is doubtless one of the high duties of a good citizen, but it is not the highest. The laws of necessity, of self-preservation, of saving our country when in danger, are of a higher obligation.

So for what Jefferson saw as a "higher obligation" he took the step that he admitted in a private letter was "an act beyond the Constitution." He stretched the powers of the presidency beyond anything that he had previously envisioned in order to obtain the Louisiana Territory. It set an historical precedent for other presidents to expand their executive powers, especially in controlling foreign policy and making war.

On December 20, 1803, at New Orleans, France formally transferred Louisiana to the United States. It enlarged "the empire of liberty," Jefferson said, offering "an ample provision for our posterity, and a widespread field for the blessings of freedom and equal laws." He could only have

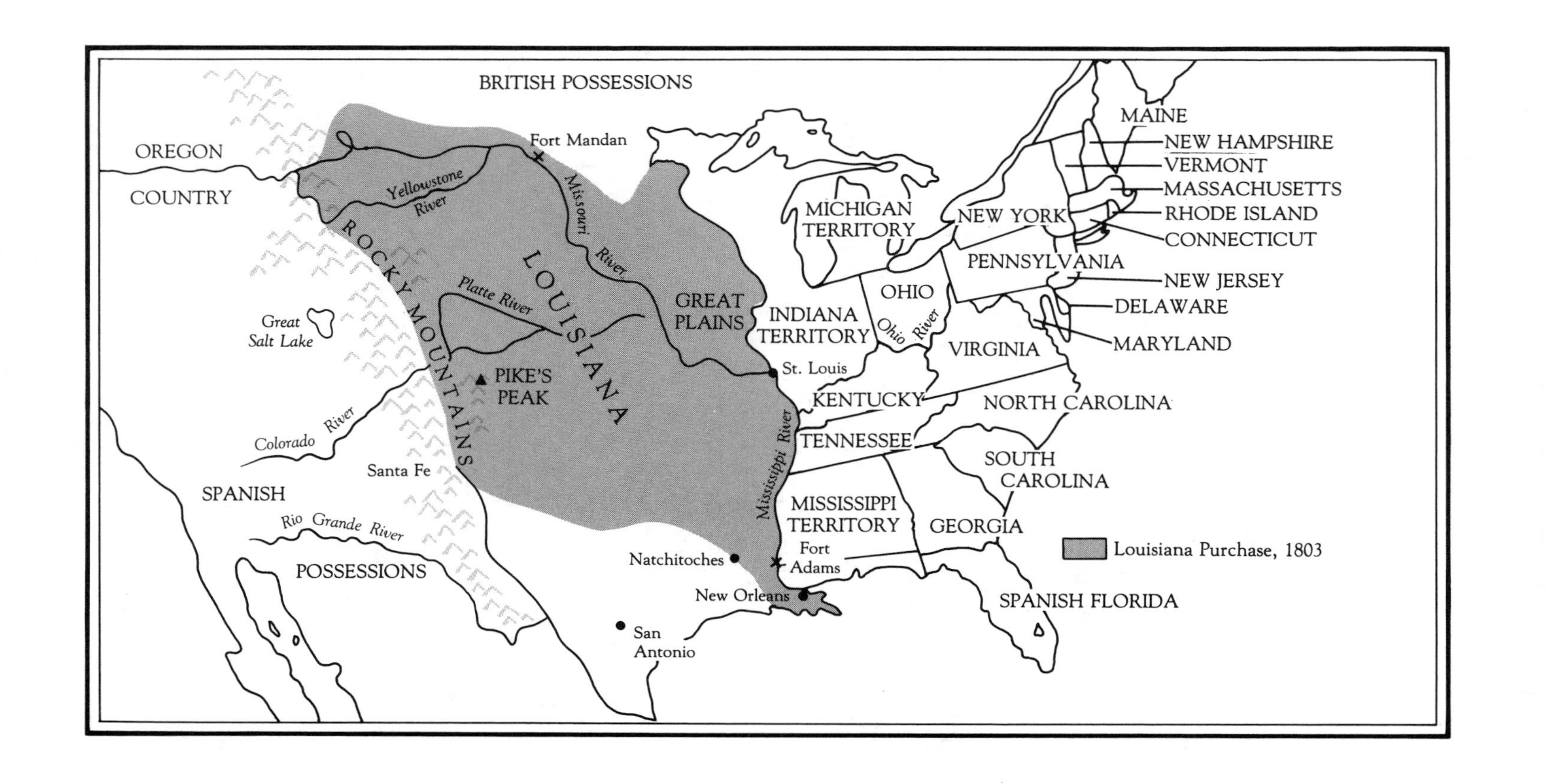
BRITISH POSSESSIONS
OREGON
COUNTRY
Fort Mandan
Yellowstone River
Missouri River
ROCKY MOUNTAINS
LOUISIANA
Platte River
Great Salt Lake
PIKE'S PEAK
GREAT PLAINS
Colorado River
Santa Fe
SPANISH
Rio Grande River
POSSESSIONS
Natchitoches
San Antonio
New Orleans
Fort Adams
Mississippi River
St. Louis
MICHIGAN TERRITORY
INDIANA TERRITORY
OHIO
Ohio River
KENTUCKY
TENNESSEE
MISSISSIPPI TERRITORY
NEW YORK
PENNSYLVANIA
VIRGINIA
NORTH CAROLINA
SOUTH CAROLINA
GEORGIA
SPANISH FLORIDA
MAINE
NEW HAMPSHIRE
VERMONT
MASSACHUSETTS
RHODE ISLAND
CONNECTICUT
NEW JERSEY
DELAWARE
MARYLAND
Louisiana Purchase, 1803

meant for white Americans; the new territory also offered a wide field for the expansion of slavery. In 1804 a northern senator proposed an amendment to the bill organizing the territory of Louisiana. It would ban slavery throughout the vast region. But Jefferson did not support it. (All that was done was to prohibit the importing of slaves into the territory from abroad.) He had lost some of the antislavery zeal that had led him, in 1784, to propose excluding slavery from all territories of the United States.

Slavery already existed, of course, in the territory of Louisiana. Perhaps Jefferson could have suggested a bargain to Congress: confirm the existence of slavery in New Orleans in exchange for making the rest of the territory free soil. As it turned out, the condition of slaves in Louisiana got worse as a result of the American takeover. They had been granted certain rights under the French code; the Americans abolished all those rights, designating the slaves as nothing but property.

In extending the western frontier from the Appalachians across the Mississippi to the Rockies, Jefferson anticipated the Indians would move there. He wanted Congress to encourage them to settle down on smaller tracts and become farmers. If they could be induced to give up hunting and go into agriculture, they would be brought into "civilization." And then, eventually, they would cede the remainder of their lands to the United States. In his vision of rugged individualism, there was no room for the Native American community and the seasonal cycles of tribal life. Later, in 1812, he would say, "The backward [tribes] will yield, and we shall be obliged to drive them, with the beasts of the forest, into the stony [Rocky] mountains."

★ 18 ★

SCANDAL

What were the western regions of the continent like? Jefferson had dreamed for the past twenty years of finding out someday. Midway in his first term he told the Spanish and the French that the American government would like permission to send an expedition through their territories to collect scientific information. When they gave him tentative approval the president asked Congress for $2,500 to fund a small expedition to explore the Missouri River to its source and to seek a water passage to the Pacific. Knowing they would want a good business motive, he said this would help expand trade with the Indians.

Granted the money, he asked the advice of his cabinet and of fellow scientists in drawing up plans and making preparations. He had already decided on Meriwether Lewis, his secretary, as leader of the expedition. The twenty-eight-year-old army captain was from his own Albemarle County, knew something of the western country, and had shown his ability to command men. Lewis asked William Clark to join him as co-leader.

Jefferson opened his large library on the practical arts and sciences to Lewis, who spent long hours in studying the history of exploration and geography. He discussed with the president what scientific data to observe and record, what equipment to gather, and how to prepare for the dangers the expedition might face. Jefferson passed on to him the advice he had gathered from experts on botany, zoology, astronomy, and medical practice in the field. Lewis also got a quick grounding in surveying and mapping.

In the spring of 1804 Lewis and Clark departed from St. Louis, heading northwest toward Oregon's Pacific shore. Their band of forty-five included soldiers, French watermen, tough Kentuckians, Clark's slave York, and Sacagawea, the Indian woman who served as translator, her baby, and her husband. They carried bales of cheap materials for gifts to the Indians—scarlet cloth, red leggings, breechclouts, burning glasses, blankets, medals, ear wire. The expedition would cost far more than the $2,500 starting money. In the end it amounted to nearly $40,000.

News of the doubling of national territory by the Louisiana Purchase and its opening up to exploration aroused great enthusiasm and added to Jefferson's popularity. Early in 1804 he announced he would stand for reelection. But his critics did not let him alone. Some Federalists went so far as to plot the secession of New England from the Union. They tried to draw Aaron Burr into the plot, but when he was defeated in a contest for the governor's chair in New York, the conspiracy collapsed.

Certainly the most painful charge repeated against Jefferson was that he had secretly fathered a large illegitimate family with one of his slaves, Sally Hemings. Although all sorts of accusations had been made against Jefferson during the presidential race of 1800, his private life had not been criticized. But halfway through his first administration, a Scottish journalist, James Callender, spread the story that Jefferson had been leading a life at Monticello so decadent that it rivaled the worst Roman emperors'.

William Clark (left) and Meriwether Lewis, leaders of the western expedition sent out by President Jefferson

A pen-and-ink sketch by Clark of a bird seen in the field during the exploration of the Louisiana Territory

Jefferson had first noticed Callender for a political pamphlet vilifying the British king and ruling class, a tract that had forced Callender to flee England under indictment for sedition. While vice president, Jefferson had made use of the man's vitriolic pen in attacks upon the Federalist leaders Adams and Hamilton, feeding him inside information and sending him money. This, though the man was an unscrupulous scandalmonger who would stoop to anything. Warned by friends not to trust Callender, Jefferson tried to conceal his cash gifts to the man but made no effort to tone down his exaggerations or falsifications.

When the printed product of this secret "collaboration" appeared, Callender was indicted under the Sedition Act, found guilty, fined, and sentenced to nine months in prison. When Jefferson became president he did not forget the journalists who had been jailed for violating the sedition law. He pardoned Callender and the others and ordered their fines to be refunded. But Callender also demanded that Jefferson make him postmaster of Richmond, Virginia. Unless he got the job, he threatened he would ruin the president's reputation with the same kinds of smears he had applied to Adams and Hamilton.

The president refused to give in to blackmail, and Callender began his attacks. In a Federalist newspaper he charged Jefferson with sexual scandal. He brought up the Walker affair of 1768 and then pictured Jefferson as the secret lover of his slave Sally Hemings and the father of five of her mulatto children. He made no investigation of the facts, never going to Monticello or trying to interview Sally or others. But the titillating story of a beautiful slave girl prostituted by the lust of an American president who then sold his offspring on the auction block was carried far and wide. Poets even published satiric verse about the scandal.

No newspaper sent reporters out to check on the charges. The investigative journalism we are familiar with today was not practiced then. Jefferson's habit, as we have seen before, was to make no response to allegations. Nor did he start legal proceedings against Callender. Early in his political career he had determined on this policy. He would not allow slander, no matter how vicious, to disturb his peace of mind. He knew that denial was no defense against character assassination. Nor did he think that any decent person, of whatever party, would believe Callender. As for the indecent ones, he cared nothing for their opinion. In a private letter to a friend, he admitted that he had made improper advances to Mrs. Walker in his youth, and then added, "It is the only one founded on truth among all the allegations against me."

Generally, Republicans did not believe the Hemings story, and Federalist politicians, savoring the chance to use these charges against Jefferson in the 1804 election, did not want to push for an investigation that might prove Callender a liar and thereby ruin a politically useful falsehood. In the summer of 1803, the body of Callender, a heavy drinker, was found in the James River. The official verdict was that he had drowned accidentally when drunk. Others thought he probably committed suicide.

You may remember that Sally Hemings entered this account of Jefferson's life in 1787. She brought his younger daughter Maria from Monticello to join her father in France. Sally was the daughter of Betty Hemings, who had been owned by John Wayles, the father of Jefferson's wife. Wayles had done what slave owners often did—make slave women like Betty their mistresses. The children born of such unions were legally slaves and could be sold. Though the practice was widespread, few planters would admit to such relationships with their slaves, and others did not talk about them. When Jefferson married, he accepted his wife's inheritance of slaves.

Sally bore five children at Monticello. If Jefferson did not father these children, who did? Much evidence points to either or both of Jefferson's nephews, Peter and Samuel Carr. They were the sons of Jefferson's sister Martha and Dabney Carr. The two young men often stayed at the Jefferson home and, as a number of sources indicate, often visited the slave quarters, where they fathered several mulatto children. The two men strongly resembled their uncle. To those who lived at Monticello, the only question was whether Peter or Samuel was the father of Sally's children.

In his will, Jefferson freed five slaves, all Hemingses. But Sally was not freed. Possibly because he felt that to have done so would have substantiated Callender's story. A few years later Jefferson's daughter Martha freed Sally; Sally lived with her sons till her death in 1835.

The charges against Jefferson were revived in the 1970s by two popular books, a biography by Fawn Brodie called *Thomas Jefferson: An Intimate Portrait* and a novel by Barbara Chase-Riboud called *Sally Hemings.* Both writers base their case largely on psychological evidence. Yet three of the leading authorities on Jefferson's life and work and several other historians, after studying all the evidence, have expressed great skepticism or outright disbelief. Not that they say Jefferson was flawless, but that fathering Sally's children has not been proved his responsibility. Readers who wish to pursue this will find the references in the bibliography.

Jefferson claimed he was running for a second term only to prove that the public did not believe the charges against him. The truth was, his party knew he was unbeatable. The Republicans dropped Vice President Burr from the ticket and put up George Clinton of New York as Jefferson's running mate. The president needed to do very little to win reelection; his record of success spoke for him. Peace, prosperity, economy in government, reduction of taxes, the acquisition of Louisiana—it was too much for the Federalists to overcome. Jefferson's party carried all but two states, tallying 163 electoral votes for him. Charles C. Pinckney, the Federalist candidate, drew only 14. Federalism was almost dead.

But if 1804 was a year of political triumph for Jefferson, privately it brought him great sorrow. Maria Eppes, his twenty-five-year-old daughter, gave birth to a girl in the spring. "A thousand joys to you, my dear Maria," Jefferson wrote when he heard the news. But Maria, depressed for a long time by the epilepsy her son Francis suffered, fell very sick herself. Jefferson hurried home as soon as Congress adjourned, hoping his presence would pull Maria through. But she died in April, and her baby soon after. Scarcely able to bear his anguish, Jefferson wrote an old friend, "Others may lose of their abundance, but I, of my want, have lost even the half of all I had. My evening prospects now hang on the slender thread of a single life." By that he meant his only surviving child, Martha. He feared even this sturdy daughter might die, breaking "this last chord of parental affection."

Other deaths that year had a significant impact on Jefferson. His older sister Mary, long plagued by marriage to an alcoholic husband, died in January. In July, Aaron Burr challenged Alexander Hamilton and killed him with a single shot in a duel on the Jersey shore of the Hudson. The bullet ended the life of Jefferson's greatest rival as well as the political career of Burr. Though he still had seven months of his vice presidential term to serve, from now on he could only plot secretly against Jefferson and his country.

★ 19 ★

SECOND-TERM ORDEAL

In great contrast to the success of his first term, Jefferson's next four years in office became a painful ordeal that ended in calamity. As with any president, external circumstances shaped in part the course of his administration. Still, in making his own decisions, he failed to do the right thing at critical moments.

On March 5, 1805, he was inaugurated president for the second time. There was little fuss; many in Congress had left for home, and he spoke in so low a voice that not half of what he said could be heard. In the inaugural address he gave special attention to the Native Americans. He praised them for their ardent love of liberty and independence, while regretting they were now being overwhelmed by the relentless drive west of white settlers. He said he was doing all he could to save them from extinction. But how? By asking them to give up their own culture and assimilate to the ways of the whites.

It was early in his second term—on September 23, 1806—that Lewis and Clark ended their triumphant journey. The reports of their exploration of the new domain heightened American interest in the West. When they proved the feasibility of an overland route to the Pacific they soon had many followers. They dealt in a friendly way with the numerous Indian tribes through whose territories they passed. Most of the Indians had no notion of the growing power of the United States and what its encroachment on their lands would do to their way of life.

Another landmark in western exploration under Jefferson's administration was the journey of Lieutenant Zebulon Pike from St. Louis up the Mississippi to chart the river and the countryside and to buy military posts from the Indians. Pike's journal and maps would become the basis for future expeditions. He followed the first with another into New Mexico and Colorado, where he explored and named Pike's Peak.

In his annual message of 1807, Jefferson reminded the Congress that the Constitution had banned interference with the slave trade for twenty years and that that period was about to close. He recommended the trade be abolished with a law that would take effect on January 1, 1808. The Congress soon adopted his proposal. This, although Jefferson's party represented the slaveholders and was in control of the Congress. Behind their approval was the fact that even with the quick spread of cotton plantations there was a surplus, not a shortage, of slaves in the country. Only South Carolina still permitted the entry of slaves from outside the country. The areas that had too many slaves, chiefly the old tobacco belt of the upper South, wanted to cut off importation so that they could sell their surplus slaves to meet the growing labor needs of the cotton planters.

Jefferson believed that ending the slave trade would mean progress on the road to abolition of slavery itself. But it only made Americans feel good. Slavery was not weakened; it tightened its grip on the life of the South. Nor was the prohibition fully effective. Congress—remember states' rights?—left it to the individual states to enforce the law. It meant slave runners of all nationalities continued to bring thousands of slaves into the country. Nevertheless, the legal ending of the trade, though not fully enforced, did save untold numbers of Africans from servitude on American plantations.

Jefferson continued to speak eloquently of freedom of the press. At the same time, he urged state officials to prosecute for sedition editors critical of his policies or of himself. Perhaps to soften the attack, he added that he hoped public anger against libelous practices by journalists would be enough to discourage them.

From the beginning of his second term Jefferson was forced to give more and more time to European affairs. He expressed his foreign policy in a famous phrase: "Peace, commerce, and honest friendship with all nations; entangling alliances with none." In Jefferson's view, England was America's prime enemy. And France, now under Napoleon's dictatorial rule, was no longer seen as a great friend. The president wanted to protect America's overseas commerce in a time of continuing war in Europe. He hoped to break free of America's long dependence on the continent. But equally important was his desire to maintain peace. Not because he was a pacifist, but because he believed war would do great harm to America's economy and to republican liberty.

Still, when necessary, he was ready to use force. In his first term he had sent naval ships to the Mediterranean to defend American shipping from the pirate states of North Africa. And now, in 1805, he had brought that war to an end with a peace treaty favorable to the United States.

When war between England and France was renewed in 1803, it created a crisis for America. Each of the two great powers tried to damage the other by cutting off its commerce, a strategy that threatened to ruin America's overseas trade. As a neutral, America traded with all nations. Not only did her sailing ships carry American exports, but they were the favorite carriers for the merchandise of South

America, the West Indies, and the Far East. The merchant marine had grown rapidly: more ships, and more sailors at such good wages that British seamen had become naturalized American citizens in order to enjoy the superior conditions on American vessels.

But this brought on unexpected trouble. In 1807 the British frigate *Leopard* fired on the American frigate *Chesapeake,* killing three men and wounding eighteen. The British took four alleged deserters from the Americans, claiming them as Britons. There is no sure way of knowing how many Americans were thus impressed by the British, but it was easily in the thousands. The *Chesapeake* incident roused Americans to fury. It could have meant war, but Jefferson did not want that. Instead he ordered British ships to stay out of American waters, demanded an apology for the attack on the *Chesapeake,* and an end to impressment.

To England, America was still only "an insignificant and puny power." She would not let this upstart nation interfere with her control of the seas.

Knowing America had too small an army and navy to fight a war, Jefferson decided on a strategy of economic coercion. He figured that American trade was so vital to the nations of Europe that he would not need to fight for what he wanted. Let's cut off our trade, he thought, and they will surely do as we wish. So at the end of 1807 he got Congress, by a large majority, to pass a law barring American vessels from sailing for any foreign port until America's rights were recognized and respected.

Did the Embargo Act work? It amounted to a self-blockade and it failed miserably. England and France would not be frightened into a change of policy. They believed it quite unlikely that their economies could be seriously damaged by the loss of American trade. And in that same time, wouldn't the embargo ruin the American commerce it was meant to protect? It was a case of cutting off your nose to spite your face.

Certainly that was how American merchants quickly came to see the embargo. Their ships idled at the wharves, their merchandise piled high in the warehouses, thousands of seamen and longshoremen had to be laid off. The planters and farmers who raised the cotton, tobacco, wheat, rice, corn, and livestock had no place to sell their surplus. In that one year of 1808 the value of American exports dropped by nearly 80 percent and imports dropped by nearly one-half. America was suffering far more than her customers.

Up and down the Atlantic coast, people openly challenged the embargo and opposed efforts to enforce it. Large amounts of American goods were smuggled out. A spirit of lawlessness spread as the government took increasingly harsh measures. Farmers and laborers who had supported the Jeffersonians deserted the party. Resolutions of protest flooded into Washington. In New England, people once again began talking of seceding from the Union.

Not everyone felt that way. Across the Appalachians the western settlers suspected the British were arming the Indians and pushing them toward war. This embargo is not enough, they cried; let's get tough and take Canada away from the British.

The enormous pressure on Jefferson generated by his embargo dominated his last year in office. It led him to acts that conflicted with his basic ideas on how good government works. For so eloquent a statesman it is surprising that he never made out a clear case for the embargo with either Congress or the public. Like many politicians who've made serious mistakes, the worse things got, the more he committed himself to bad policy. At his request Congress gave him unprecedented and unconstitutional powers to enforce the embargo. It let him interfere with the way everyone did business. He became "so obsessed with the immediate problem of making the Embargo work," wrote Dumas Malone, "as to be unmindful of republican theory and also of certain basic facts of human nature."

Cartoon of a merchant trying to smuggle goods out of the country during Jefferson's disastrous embargo of foreign trade. The merchant is nipped by a turtle symbolizing government authority.

In the name of the embargo, said Forrest McDonald, "Jefferson conducted a fifteen-month reign of oppression and repression that was unprecedented in American history and would not be matched for another 110 years, when Jefferson's ideological heir Woodrow Wilson occupied the presidency."

The president tried to stop resistance to the law by force, using both the state militia and the regular army. He declared the whole region of Lake Champlain to be in a state of insurrection because a few smugglers were defying the embargo. In May he said he would suppress all domestic commerce conducted only for profit. Which meant he would ruin the livelihood of tens of thousands of sailors, fishermen, whalers, shippers, and merchants. That policy was challenged at once in the courts and a Supreme Court justice,

The English laughed at Jefferson in this political cartoon, the satire of which is directed at the Embargo Act and its harmful effects on American merchants. The Emperor Napoleon stands behind Jefferson, saying "You shall be King hereafter." The merchants in front of Jefferson complain while the president spouts only grand theory.

one of his own Republican appointees, ruled the president had exceeded his authority. Jefferson simply ignored the high court's decision. In June militiamen captured a large raft of lumber on Lake Champlain, only to have it retaken by a band of lumberjacks. Jefferson had five of the men arrested and charged with treason, but a Republican judge acquitted them and angrily denounced the indictment itself.

Frustrated when court rulings went against him, Jefferson decided judges and juries could not be trusted. Instead of going to court, he began to rely more and more on martial law and the armed forces. His navy, supposed to protect American shipping, was soon being used against that shipping. Without any legal authority, he ordered the regular army to act as a police force. Soon most of the northern frontier was under control of the army.

Such extreme measures did not quell civil disobedience. Pitched battles were fought and scores of people wounded or killed. As Congress assembled in November, Jefferson had placed whole towns under taint of treason. He even reminded one congressman that in times of emergency, "the universal resource is a dictator."

So in its attempt to avoid war with Europe, the Jefferson administration was making war upon its own people. And all for what? The net effect on the international economy was so slight that Europeans felt only contempt for the policy.

Still, Jefferson must be given credit for not rushing into war under great provocation. He tried to use peaceful sanctions against Britain and France. There was no historical example to prove it could work, for economic pressure on so great a scale had never been tried before. What he did not foresee was that Americans were not willing to suffer deep economic distress for a national policy. An embargo for an unlimited period required their cooperation and sacrifice. Yet Jefferson imposed his policy without any effort to secure public understanding. He refused to listen to criticism, tolerated no opposition, and used terrible means to gain his ends. Perhaps because of his first term, he was so used to getting Congress to do whatever he asked that he had come to expect support simply out of faith in him as president.

The embargo failed to force the European powers to end their harassment of American commerce. And at home its crippling effects on the economy and on personal and property rights threatened to split Jefferson's own party. Fearing the possible loss of political power, the Jeffersonians in Congress voted to end the embargo on March 4, 1809—Jefferson's last day in office.

Early in his second term Jefferson had confided to close friends that he would follow Washington's precedent and not seek a third term. However, Republicans, worried over their party's slide in public favor, urged him not to retire. As the pressure mounted, Jefferson felt obliged to stop it. He said that although the Constitution placed no time limit on a president's service, he feared the office could become one for life. And he believed that no crisis, domestic or foreign, could justify hanging on to the presidency. Undergoing the agony of the embargo only strengthened his feeling. Like many presidents, he felt physically and spiritually exhausted at the end of a second term.

His flat no opened the way for a successor. Madison, his secretary of state and his personal choice, was nominated by the Republicans. He won comfortably over the Federalist candidate, although that party did well in local and state elections. Now Jefferson could leave office with his party and policies still in control and his closest friend as head of the government.

In the months between the election and March, when his presidency would end, the president all but gave up political leadership. He began packing his things and sending them home to Monticello. He had long looked forward to retirement and could hardly wait. Near the end, he wrote a friend, "Within a few days I retire to my family, my books and farms. . . . Never did a prisoner, released from his chains, feel such relief as I shall on shaking off the shackles of power." Anticipating his return to Monticello, he wrote another friend, "I am full of plans of employment when I get there—they chiefly respect the active functions of the body. To the mind I still administer amusement chiefly. An only daughter and numerous family of grandchildren will furnish my great resources of happiness."

On Inauguration Day, Jefferson stood beside Madison as Chief Justice Marshall administered the oath of office to the new president. He stayed in Washington a week more, then left the capital forever. He mounted his horse and rode through harsh winter weather for three days and nights until he reached Monticello. Never again would he leave his beloved home.

★ 20 ★

PLEASURES AND SORROWS

Jefferson was nearly sixty-six when he left Washington for the last time. Now he would be able to do whatever he liked. Monticello—forty years since he had begun building it—was nearly completed. His daughter Martha had come there several days before to put it in order. He expected his family to come live with him, and that was what they wanted too. At thirty-seven, Martha had had eight children, and four more would come in quick order.

From his neighbors Jefferson got a warm welcome. They were happy to have their eminent friend home again, and this time to stay. Children of old friends came to visit, joining the family in dancing to the music of a slave fiddler. Scholars and scientists dropped in at Monticello as well, to talk with Jefferson about their diverse projects. Soon, however, the steady stream of visitors became a burden. Strangers climbed the hill just to gawk at the grand old man who had helped create their republic, and others to ask his advice on things political or personal.

One of those who visited Jefferson was Edward Coles, a young neighbor who had been private secretary to James

Madison. He called on Jefferson to put his great prestige behind the antislavery movement. Only such eminent leaders as you can arouse public sentiment to do the right thing, he said. As for Coles himself, he had decided to sell his estate in Virginia and, taking his slaves with him, move to the free soil of Illinois, where he would settle the blacks as free people on farms.

Expecting approval, he was jolted when Jefferson said the experiment would fail. Blacks simply were as "incapable as children of taking care of themselves." He advised Coles to stay in Virginia and work "softly but steadily" toward eventual emancipation. He would pray for Coles, but nothing more.

Coles went ahead on his own and settled nineteen freed slaves as tenant farmers in Illinois, giving them an opportunity to gain ownership of 160-acre tracts on easy terms.

Jefferson was too polite to turn anyone away, and often provided beds for overnight. Martha recalled that as many as fifty people might be staying with them at one time, some sleeping in borrowed beds. In the face of all this, Jefferson tried to stick to his daily routine. He continued to rise at daybreak, spending hours answering his mail. Letters poured in asking for job references, encouragement for new inventions, advice on scientific matters, reminiscences for historical research, not to mention extensive correspondence with old friends and political co-workers. Pausing for breakfast, he would then mount his horse to inspect his plantations with his overseer. At about four came dinner with the family and guests. Then, until dark, he chatted with friends. At candlelight he went to bed, reading until sleep took him.

One of the great pleasures of retirement was the time it gave him to work with his hands. He always had his tool chest with him, whether in the White House or here at home. Isaac, one of his slaves, who had often seen Jefferson at work with tools, recalled that he was as "neat a hand as ever you saw to make keys and locks and small chains, iron and brass."

Martha Jefferson Randolph, the president's longest surviving child, painted by Thomas Sully

Although the mansion was pretty well completed, his restless inventiveness had him devising changes or improvements, such as a new way to fireproof the ceilings, or a way to redesign windows and interior doors for better weatherproofing. These were but a few of dozens of innovations; most worked, some failed. Outdoors, he applied his knowledge of chemistry to farming, trying always to make Monticello self-sufficient. His ideas found application in brewing, distilling, drainage, ice making, fencing, gunpowder, building materials, in designing his own apple mill as well as his carriages. He used his telescope to make astronomical observations and designed a spherical sundial too.

A hint of the delights of private life comes in a letter he wrote his Revolutionary War friend, General Thaddeus Kosciusko, of Poland. Now he could freely "talk of ploughs and harrows, of seeding and harvesting, with my neighbors, and of politics too, if they choose, with as little reserve as the rest of my fellow citizens, and feel, at length, the blessing of being free to say and do what I please without being responsible for it to any mortal."

Odd as it may seem to us, back some 200 years ago Jefferson was mindful of the need to conserve the earth's resources. He had learned the hard way how plain neglect and poor management could ruin his lands in the long years of his absence. He had seen how the repeated plantings of staple crops like tobacco and corn could exhaust the soil. It had cost him much when the red soil of his farms was washed away by erosion. Happily he was able to arrest such deterioration when he began contour plowing with the use of a hillside plow that his son-in-law Thomas Mann Randolph had designed. "The spontaneous energies of the earth are a gift of nature," he said, suggesting that we should all strive not to waste that gift for quick profits but to conserve it for humanity.

A letter he wrote to Charles W. Peale, his artist friend,

in praise of farming reveals his attachment to the earth and its gifts:

> I have often thought that if heaven had given me choice of my position and calling, it should have been on a rich spot of earth, well watered, and near a good market for the production of the garden. No occupation is so delightful to me as the culture of the earth, and no culture comparable to that of the garden. Such a variety of subjects, some one always coming to perfection, the failure of one thing repaired by the success of another, and instead of one harvest a continued one throughout the year.

In his late sixties, his white crown of hair signified old age. But his health was good, and his strength reinforced by an active life. His overseer, Edmund Bacon, said that this 6-foot, 2½-inch man was "straight as a gun barrel," and "like a fine horse, he had no surplus flesh." A visitor from Washington at this time noted he was full of "enthusiasm, ardor and gaiety."

But it would not last long. Nearing seventy, he felt the "hand of age" upon him. As every year passed he lost something physically. His sight faded, then his hearing. And next, he said, "something else will be going, until all is gone." He even believed his mind had weakened, a loss no one else could detect. But it did not anger or depress him. This was only the natural and inevitable process of decay. Everything had its time, and so did he.

In his early seventies Jefferson handed his eldest and most capable grandson, Jeff Randolph, the management of his farms in Albemarle. By this time Jefferson had twelve grandchildren. The older ones were girls, to whom he was very generous. He would take one or two of them with him on the three-day journey to his 5,000-acre estate at Poplar Forest in Bedford County. It was near Lynchburg, and 90 miles from Monticello. The compact house he had built there was a sanctuary where he could be free of unwanted visitors. The two-story house was an architectural gem he had designed in the form of an octagon while president.

It may sound like a happy, carefree life in retirement, but chopping away at his peace of mind was the heavy ax of debt. In public service he had added nothing to his private income (unlike many in high office who have used their privileged position and power to build considerable private wealth). Quite the contrary. He had run up debt of $10,000 while president, a huge sum in those days, and knew he would have to sell off large tracts of land to pay his debts. He hoped to be able to hang on to enough property to help his grandchildren as they tried to gain a secure foothold in adult life. But his daughter Martha, taking over management of Monticello, insisted that his needs must come first. "I can bear anything but the idea of seeing you harassed in your old age by debts or deprived of those comforts which long habit has rendered necessary to you. The possession of millions would not compensate for one year's sadness and discomfort to you."

Do what he could, the debts only mounted higher. Jefferson's fields were never productive enough to be profitable. The land was poor, uneven, hard to work, afflicted by drought and pests. In the end, debt would crush all his hopes for the family's future.

Aging, however, did not diminish his interest in public affairs. He kept in close touch with the Virginia friends who succeeded him in the presidency—Madison and Monroe. They told him what was going on, sure that he would never publicly disclose or criticize their confidential exchanges.

What he had long expected and feared soon came to pass. England and America plunged into another bloody conflict. As though foretelling the political disaster, the most devastating earthquake ever recorded in North America "shook out the country like a rug," in the words of the poet Robert Penn Warren. Its epicenter was in New Madrid, Missouri. The colossal shock struck at 2 A.M. on December 16, 1811, while settlers and Indians were asleep in the frontier village on the bank of the Mississippi. Tremors shook the earth almost continuously for months, especially in the Ohio and Mississippi valleys, causing an incalculable loss of life and property.

By weird coincidence, that same night two of Jefferson's nephews, Lilburne and Isham Lewis, the sons of his sister Lucy Lewis, murdered a teenage slave named George, the body servant and handyman of one of the brothers. The killing was done for no offense, and in a horrifyingly brutal way. While out on bail awaiting trial, Lilburne committed suicide and Isham fled, disappearing. The murder was widely reported in the press, but Jefferson never referred to it. He couldn't bring himself to discuss or face the appalling episode, perhaps because it revealed what was possible in people of his own blood.

In the brief time leading up to the War of 1812, Jefferson's successor, President Madison, tried various maneuvers to shape British policy to America's advantage. Nothing worked. Britain only stepped up its campaign of impressment of sailors and seizure of American ships. Of course it heightened America's war fever. A new group of congressmen from the West and South began calling loudly for war. They claimed the government was doing little to protect the interests of its citizens and to uphold the nation's honor. Jefferson was one of those who welcomed the war. He saw it as a second war for American independence. Foolishly, he was sure the Americans would walk all over the British and conquer Canada, thereby adding enormously to U.S. territory. The intense pressure led Madison in June 1812 to ask Congress for a declaration of war.

It was a strange war. The causes were cloudy and the goals vague. The cocky Americans failed to capture Canada.

They succeeded only in proving how bad American military leaders were. The British attacked south from Canada and, marching inland, occupied Washington, burning the Capitol and the President's Mansion. (It got the name the White House after being repaired and painted white.) The president, the Congress, and the army fled into Virginia.

Luckily, Britain proved too busy fighting Napoleon's armies in Europe to follow up on her success. Meanwhile American quarrels over the war got so intense that a terrible riot broke out in Baltimore, with Republicans and Federalists fighting in the streets, and enraged mobs beating or shooting people to death. It was a frightening sign of how high emotions ran between the War Hawks of the West and South and the antiwar groups in New England and the Middle Atlantic region. The five New England states met in Hartford to debate proposals for secession from the Union. Wiser heads prevailed, luckily, although the convention did insist on the right of a state to nullify acts of the federal government that it considered unconstitutional. This was Jefferson's old belief, coming home to haunt him.

The war ended on Christmas Eve of 1814, when terms of a peace treaty were agreed upon. The war was really a draw, which was why the treaty settled little; it simply ended the fighting while joint commissions were set up to deal with the remaining disputes. What the war did do, however, was to relieve Americans of the fear of outside attacks upon their Republic. We won, people said, so the country seemed secure to them at last.

Months after the war's end Jefferson learned that in the British devastation of the Capitol, the congressional library had been burned. Every book was gone. At once he made suggestions for rebuilding the library and offered to sell his own collection of books to it. After a lifetime of collecting, he owned nearly 6,500 volumes, many of them rare and valuable, purchased abroad as he hunted through Europe for everything relating to America.

Congress decided to accept his proposal, paying prices based solely on the physical size of each book. The sum came to $23,950, only a fraction of the true value. He shipped his books to Washington in ten wagonloads. The librarians arranged them on a classification system developed by Jefferson, a system that was continued into the 1900s.

The money Jefferson received gave him temporary relief from his debts. More important was the great contribution he made to American civilization. Although he never claimed he had founded the Library of Congress, in reality it was his book collection that became the invaluable core of what would rank as one of the world's greatest national institutions.

By this time Jefferson's party, the Republicans, had triumphed over the Federalists, who were broken as a national political force. Many of the Federalists, however, were finding common ground with northern Jeffersonian Republicans who opposed slavery. No one party could contain the nation's growing diversity. Clashing economic and social interests powered the sectional differences that were dividing the country. The Missouri crisis of 1819–20 showed how deep-seated the sectional split had become. Central to the split was the explosive issue of slavery.

It erupted when Congress began a bitter and passionate debate over the extension of slavery into the territories. Missouri's application for admission to the Union raised the question of slavery's expansion. Congress had to decide what to do about the vast new territory acquired by Jefferson's Louisiana Purchase. Jefferson and the Southerners demanded the Congress not close the territory to their slave property. He predicted the most dreadful consequences for American if the spread of slavery were checked. His region insisted on maintaining the balance between the slave and free states in the Senate. But northerners wanted to keep the trans-Mississippi West open to free labor, and closed to slavery.

For three months the debate raged in the Congress. "This momentous question," said Jefferson, "like a fire-bell in the night, awakened and filled me with terror." At seventy-seven when he wrote those words, his optimism had given way to pessimism. He thought the bell was tolling the end of the Union. Where once he had predicted a racial war of extermination between whites and blacks, now he believed the end of the nation would come in the form of a civil war between North and South over slavery.

The debate was stilled for a time by the passage of the Missouri Compromise of 1820. Missouri came into the Union as a slave state, and Maine as a free state. So the sectional balance was maintained, at twelve states each. The informal line barring slavery from all new states north of the Ohio River, however, had now been advanced to the lands west of the Mississippi. Sadly, the Jefferson who back in 1784 had tried to exclude slavery from the territories, now stood for the unlimited expansion of slavery in the territories.

In taking this stand on the Missouri crisis, Jefferson pleased the planters who had been angered by the antislavery views of his *Notes on Virginia.* Heavily in debt now, he was hard pressed to make slave labor pay. To keep the slaves housed, clothed, and fed was expensive, and to overcome their natural resistance to being sweated for no pay was even harder. Here he was, supervising daily a system he hated while realizing his livelihood depended on its continuation. It sometimes made him morally callous. The slaves became mere objects of financial calculation. He anticipated modern time-and-motion studies by measuring scientifically the amount of time needed to perform a particular task and then holding his slaves strictly to it. He talked of the fertility of his female slaves as though they were livestock. "I consider a woman who brings a child every two years as more profitable than the best man of the farm; what she produces is an addition to the capital, while his labors disappear in mere consumption."

The coldness of this view some attribute to Jefferson's growing fear of financial collapse. His last years were a race between bankruptcy and death, with his creditors gaining steadily. Today we take for granted that former presidents are paid handsome pensions and expenses and allowed a staff. But that practice did not begin until 1958. Jefferson had no financial help from any source. (The nation did better for its foreign friends. Lafayette, for his service in the Revolution, was given $200,000 by Congress when he visited America in 1824–25.)

Little would occur in his declining years to change Jefferson's bleak view of America's future—except for the fulfillment of his old dream of establishing a great university. A quarter of a century before, he had begun to make plans for what would become the University of Virginia. It was to be the crowning point of a state system of education from elementary school to college. He believed that intelligence and ability were "sown as liberally among the poor as the rich." The best way to discover such talent was through common education open to all. Those with promise would be helped to develop themselves in the university. His thinking, as we've seen, made no room for releasing the talents blocked by racism. Nor did he ever develop a plan for educating women.

When Jefferson failed to move the state legislature to support public schools, he turned to planning the university and to lobbying the lawmakers to carry out his ideas. In 1816 they passed a bill Jefferson had drawn up putting himself, Madison, and Monroe on a board with others to acquire land and design the university. At its first meeting the board elected Jefferson rector of the university.

Jefferson himself drew the architectural plans and took on the job of builder. He conceived the entirely novel idea of creating an "academic village" with dormitories for students adjoining pavilions where the professors would live and hold classes. He surveyed the land, staked out the terraces and pavilions, and had the cornerstone of the first pavilion laid. Stubbornly he kept pushing the legislature to establish a complete state system of education. But the members would

A view of the University of Virginia, Jefferson's "Academic Village." It is located two miles from Monticello, which is faintly visible atop the mountain, right of center.

not act, failing to understand, as he put it, "that knowledge is power, that knowledge is safety, that knowledge is happiness."

Certainly he found happiness in planning every detail of the university. He proposed the subjects to be taught, the kind of faculty he desired, the bylaws for operation. His aim was high: to build "an institution where science in all its branches is taught, and in the highest degree to which the human mind has carried it." (By "science" he meant all knowledge.) The faculty was to be top-rank, drawn from Europe if Americans of equal caliber could not be enlisted.

Getting funds out of the legislature to accomplish his goals proved difficult. He let it be known that other states were spending more than Virginia on education. He appealed to state and regional pride to at least match their standards. He played on the intense sectional feelings aroused by the Missouri issue and asked whether Virginians wanted to trust their sons to be educated in northern schools by "those who are against us in position and principle." Do we want Harvard or Princeton professors "to fashion to their own form the minds of our youth?"

Lack of funds slowed both construction and the hiring of faculty. Not until 1824 were the buildings ready for use and funds put up to buy books and equipment. While an agent searched for faculty in Europe and America, Jefferson drafted schedules for classes, rules for student conduct, requirements for exams and for awarding degrees, and submitted these to the board for approval.

When it came to selecting texts for the students to use, Jefferson broke with his advocacy of an institution "to be based on the illimitable freedom of the human mind. For here we are not afraid to follow truth wherever it may lead, nor to tolerate any error so long as reason is left free to combat it." He wanted the students to read those specific authorities whose point of view he endorsed. The faculty too must be "politically sound."

As the work on the university neared completion, Lafayette arrived in America to enjoy a celebration in his honor unmatched in American history. The French hero reached Monticello in November 1824 and stayed for ten days. The two old friends had not seen each other for some thirty-five years, since the first days of the French revolution. They burst into tears as they embraced. At a ceremonial dinner for Lafayette held in the Rotunda of the university, Jefferson was toasted as "the founder of the University of Virginia." Too feeble of voice to speak, he had his remarks read for him. He praised Lafayette and thanked his friends and neighbors for their kindnesses over the years. He wished success for the university, and for the "indissoluble union" of his beloved country. It was his last public speech.

In March 1825 the university opened. Everyone praised the founder for his magnificent creation. A visiting professor from Harvard said the buildings were more beautiful than any architecture in New England, and perhaps the best for a university that could be found anywhere in the world. Jefferson kept his hand on campus affairs until the end of his life. It was one of the three great achievements of his life that he wished to be remembered for.

★ 21 ★

DEBT AND DEATH

As he entered his eighties, the magnitude of his debts frightened Jefferson. For a time he thought of selling eighty of his slaves, while keeping one hundred and fifty others. But he changed his mind and sent only four to the auction block. His poor health further depressed his spirits. He suffered badly from enlargement of the prostate gland and rheumatism, and had to take to his bed quite often. Family life was a mixture of sorrow and joy. There were marriages and births to celebrate but debts burdening his sons-in-law involved Jefferson as well. When his daughter Martha had to sell some of her domestic slaves it led her to write, "The discomfort of slavery I have borne all my life, but its sorrows in all their bitterness I never before perceived. Nothing can prosper under such a system of injustice."

Near the end, illness forced Jefferson permanently to bed. He received an invitation to come to Washington to celebrate the fiftieth anniversary of the signing of the Declaration of Independence. He could not go, he wrote, but he hoped the choice made that Fourth of July in 1776 would be "the signal to arouse people to break the chains of ignorance

A portrait of Jefferson by Thomas Sully

and superstition that bound them, and to assume the blessing and security of self-government. . . . The mass of mankind," he said, "has not been born with saddles on their backs, nor a favored few booted and spurred, ready to ride them. . . ."

One of the blessings of these last years came about through the reunion of Jefferson and his old friend John Adams. For the last twenty-five years of their lives the two never saw one another face to face. After their painful break at the end of the Adams administration in 1801, they did not exchange a single letter until 1812. It was Dr. Benjamin Rush, the warm friend of both, who appealed to them as fellow signers of the Declaration of Independence to embrace once again. Finally, on New Year's Day of 1812, Adams wrote Jefferson a short note, and Jefferson replied with an affectionate letter recalling their earlier years together.

It opened a brilliant correspondence—158 letters in all—full of ideas, of passionate feelings, of humor and wit, of books and history, of religion and philosophy. They talked wonderfully on paper about man, society, and themselves. The rich correspondence shows markedly different personalities, sometimes agreeing, sometimes disputing, but always devoted to the pursuit of truth.

In one letter Adams asked Jefferson if he would live his life over again. Yes, said Jefferson, he would—except for the last sickly years. He believed the world to be a good one on the whole, dealing out more pleasure than pain. "My temperament is sanguine," he said. "I steer my bark with Hope in the head, leaving Fear astern."

Adams, on the other hand, was skeptical about human beings and their progress. He thought the rights of mankind were no more fully attainable than human perfection. "We must come to the principles of Jesus," he wrote. "But when will all men and all nations do as they would be done by?"

Jefferson's own view of life and the way to live it came in part from his reading of Greek and Roman thinkers. He

A ticket for the unsuccessful public lottery launched in 1826 to help the dying Jefferson meet his heavy debts

wrote his old secretary William Short that happiness is the aim of life, and virtue the foundation of happiness. The active, self-disciplined life, he said, is the best means to happiness. From the Roman poet Horace he copied into a notebook the famous words of advice: "Enjoy the day and put as little trust as possible in the morrow." But it was in the ethics of Jesus, as we saw earlier, that he found the best guide to the good life.

As 1826 came on, Jefferson thought of an idea to solve all his financial problems. If he could sell a large part of his lands, it would bring in the money he desperately needed. But how, at a time when land values were dreadfully low? The answer: to hold a lottery throughout the Union, selling about 11,000 tickets at $10 each. The winners would get land as their reward. His grandson Jeff liked the idea and took on the task of moving it ahead. When word got out to the public, however, many feared it would ruin Jefferson's reputation. It was a form of gambling, of speculation, after all, and hadn't he opposed that? But the legislature reluctantly gave it the necessary approval. Jefferson still felt uneasy; if it didn't work, he would have to sell Monticello itself.

As late as June, lottery tickets had not yet been put on sale. In New York, it was proposed that the community buy lottery tickets and then destroy them on the Fourth of July. Some friends tried to raise funds as gifts to deliver Jefferson from all his debts. Admirers in New York sent in $7,500. But the contributions from all sources were far too small to meet his obligations. On July 4, 1826, no lottery tickets were destroyed because none had yet been sold.

And that was the day Jefferson died. He had sunk very low in the last week of June. His doctor stayed with him, knowing there was no chance of recovery. The family were summoned to hurry home. Until the last few days Jefferson's mind was clear and calm. He lost consciousness the night of July 2. Waking for a moment, he asked if this was the Fourth of July. Soon it will be, he was told. As the clock reached a minute past midnight to begin the Fourth, the family at the bedside were gratified that Jefferson had lived until the day he made so glorious in history. He died at fifty minutes after the noon hour.

It was a remarkable coincidence that on that same fiftieth anniversary of the signing of the Declaration of Independence, his fellow signer John Adams died too. The old man's last words were: "Thomas Jefferson still survives."

Jefferson was buried the next day at Monticello, beside his wife. A slave made the coffin, and another slave dug the grave. Family and slaves carried him to his resting place, where neighbors and University of Virginia students said their last good-bye.

In the will he drew up a few months before his death, Jefferson left his estate in trust to his daughter Martha. He gave a walking stick to Madison, watches to all his grandchildren, and his books to the university. Freedom was granted to three of his adult male slaves, and two others were to be freed on reaching maturity. All five had trades which could support them. His grandson Jeff Randolph he made his executor, leaving him all of his business and personal papers. The correspondence alone consisted of 40,000 letters.

The entrance to Jefferson's home, restored after long years of neglect following his death in 1826. "All my wishes end where I hope my days will end, at Monticello," he once said.

A few years later, the great house at Monticello and many of the Jefferson slaves were sold on the auction block. The amount realized was not enough to meet the family debts. Jefferson's grandson Thomas Jefferson Randolph paid the $40,000 deficit out of his own pocket.

On the plain obelisk he had designed to mark his grave were inscribed the words he had written:

Here was buried
Thomas Jefferson
Author of the Declaration of Independence
of the Statute of Virginia for religious freedom
and father of the University of Virginia

These were what he wished most to be remembered by.

★ ★ ★

A NOTE ON SOURCES

There is an enormous amount of material on Jefferson and his times. The best way to begin is to read what he had to say for himself. Publication of the definitive edition of his own writings was begun in 1950 by the editor Julian P. Boyd, in *The Papers of Thomas Jefferson,* Princeton. To date twenty-four volumes have been issued with at least as many more to come. The latest takes Jefferson through 1792, and the man lived another thirty-four years.

One-volume selections include *The Life and Selected Writings of Thomas Jefferson,* edited by Adrienne Koch and William Peden, Modern Library, 1944, and Merrill D. Peterson's *Thomas Jefferson: Writings,* Library of America, 1984. Eight of Jefferson's most important documents are in Richard Hofstadter's *Great Issues in American History, 1765–1865,* Vintage, 1958.

To supplement the collected papers there are many specialized volumes that focus on a single interest. Among them are *The Adams-Jefferson Letters,* edited by Lester Cappon, University of North Carolina, 1954; and *The Family Letters of Thomas Jefferson,* edited by Edwin M. Betts and James A.

Bear, Jr., University of Missouri, 1966. Betts also edited *Thomas Jefferson's Garden Book, 1766–1824,* Lippincott, 1944, and *Thomas Jefferson's Farm Book,* Princeton, 1953.

The best comprehensive biography that everyone who writes on Jefferson draws upon is by Dumas Malone: *Jefferson and His Time,* Little, Brown, 1948–81. Representing the scholarship of a lifetime, it runs to six large volumes and is crammed with detail on every aspect of Jefferson's life and work. A major study in one volume is Merrill Petersen's *Thomas Jefferson and the New Nation,* Oxford University, 1970. A more recent study is Noble E. Cunningham's *In Pursuit of Reason: The Life of Thomas Jefferson,* Ballantine, 1987.

Two leading historians have given us stimulating perspectives on Jefferson: Henry Steel Commager, *Jefferson, Nationalism and the Enlightenment,* Braziller, 1975; and in chapter 2 of *The American Political Tradition and the Men Who Made It,* Vintage, 1954, Richard Hofstadter analyzes "Thomas Jefferson: The Aristocrat as Democrat."

For insight into an achievement Jefferson was so proud of, see *The Virginia Statute for Religious Freedom: Its Evolution and Consequences in American History,* edited by Merrill Petersen and Robert C. Vaughan, Cambridge University, 1988.

About the birth of the nation and Jefferson's role in it, there are many studies. I used Carl Becker's *The Declaration of Independence,* Vintage, 1958; Garry Wills, *Inventing America: Jefferson's Declaration of Independence,* Vintage, 1978; Richard B. Morris, *The Forging of the Nation, 1781–1789,* Harper, 1987; Michael Kammen, *The Origins of the American Constitution: A Documentary History,* Penguin, 1986; and Edmund S. Morgan, *The Birth of the Republic, 1763–1789,* Chicago, 1956. For Jefferson as president there is the penetrating and compact *The Presidency of Thomas Jefferson,* by Forrest McDonald, University of Kansas, 1976. A provocative study that challenges popular views is *The Radical Politics of Thomas Jefferson: A Revisionist View,* by Richard K. Matthews, University of Kansas, 1984. Among many important studies of Jefferson and foreign policy there are Walter LaFeber's *The American Age: U.S. Foreign Policy at Home and Abroad Since 1750,* Norton, 1989; and *Empire of Liberty: The Statecraft of Thomas Jefferson,* by Robert Tucker and David C. Hendrickson, Oxford University, 1990.

The best treatment of Jefferson and the Native Americans is *Seeds of Extinction: Jeffersonian Philanthropy and the American Indian,* by Bernard W. Sheehan, Norton, 1973. On Jefferson's attitude toward slavery, see John C. Miller, *The Wolf by the Ears: Thomas Jefferson and Slavery,* Free Press, 1977; chapter 12 in Winthrop Jordan, *White Over Black: American Attitudes Toward the Negro, 1550–1812,* Norton, 1977; and Robert McColley, *Slavery and Jeffersonian Virginia,* University of Illinois, 1964. Scattered insights can be found in Mechal Sobel, *The World They Made Together: Black and White Values in 18th Century Virginia,* Princeton University, 1987.

For the question of civil liberties in Jefferson's time and the way practice could contradict principle, see Leonard W. Levy, *Jefferson and Civil Liberties: The Darker Side,* Harvard University, 1963, and the essay "Jefferson as a Civil Libertarian," in Levy's *Constitutional Opinions,* Oxford University, 1986.

The charge that Jefferson had a slave as his mistress for several decades is found in the biography by Fawn Brodie, *Thomas Jefferson: An Intimate Portrait,* Norton, 1974, and in the novel by Barbara Chase-Riboud, *Sally Hemings,* Viking, 1979. These versions of the story are challenged by the historian Virginius Dabney in *The Jefferson Scandals: A Rebuttal,* Dodd, Mead, 1981. The life of the man who first published the charge, James T. Callender, one of the earliest muckraking journalists, is told in *With the Hammer of Truth,* by Michael Durey, University of Virginia, 1990.

Details and background on the murder of a slave by

Jefferson's nephews are given in Boynton Merrill, Jr., *Jefferson's Nephews: A Frontier Tragedy,* University of Kentucky, 1987.

The many facets of Jefferson's life have been examined in a variety of specialized studies. You will find books on the man's interest in or connection with art, architecture, music, philosophy, religion, education, law. There are others on the creation of Monticello, on his experience in Paris, on his library, on his portraits, on his image and influence. Among all these I would single out two volumes. One is a recent landmark study of Jefferson's lifelong concern with science, by Silvio A. Bedini, *Thomas Jefferson: Statesman of Society,* Macmillan, 1990. The other is Jack McLaughlin, *Jefferson and Monticello: The Biography of a Builder,* Holt, 1988.

The lives of those of Jefferson's contemporaries who worked with him (or against him) can be read for additional light on the man. These include such figures as Washington, Adams, Madison, Monroe, Hamilton, Burr, Lafayette, and Franklin.

Wherever possible I have listed paperback editions.

Maps by Vantage Art

Photographs courtesy of: Maryland Historical Society: Frontis, pp. 102, 107; The Jamestown Foundation: p. 17; Monticello, Thomas Jefferson Memorial Foundation, Inc.: pp. 22, 176 (middle and bottom), 177 (middle and bottom), 218; The Bettmann Archive: pp. 27, 74, 76, 90, 114, 129, 134, 171, 183, 189, 217, 223, 241; Stokes Collection, New York Public Library: p. 28; The R.W. Norton Art Gallery, Shreveport, La.: p. 33; Massachusetts Historical Society: pp. 39 (top), 45 (Coolidge Collection), 156–157, 194 (bottom); American Philosophical Society: p. 39 (bottom); Author's collection: pp. 52, 64, 194 (top); Historical Society of Pennsylvania: p. 58; Library of Congress: pp. 59, 182, 186; Yale University Art Gallery: pp. 62–63, 85; Colonial Williamsburg Foundation: pp. 80, 191; Clements Library, University of Michigan, Ann Arbor: p. 92; The Virginia State Library, Richmond: p. 99; American Antiquarian Society: pp. 105, 181; The Huntington, San Marino, Ca.: p. 115 (top); Culver Pictures: p. 115 (bottom); New York Public Library Picture Collection: pp. 124, 133, 237, 239; Independence National Historic Park: pp. 146, 147, 207 (top and middle); Art Resource: p. 149; Tracy W. McGregor Library, Special Collections Department, Manuscript Division, University of Virginia Library: p. 159 (both), 232–233; Adams National Historic Site, Quincy, Mass.: p. 167; National Museum of the American Indian: p. 176 (top); National Museum of American History, Smithsonian Institution, neg. no. 73-10283: p. 177 (top); Collection of the Supreme Court of the United States: p. 197; Missouri Historical Society, neg. no. 648: p. 207 (bottom).

INDEX

★ ★ ★

ABOUT THE AUTHOR

Milton Meltzer, distinguished biographer and historian, is the author of more than eighty books for young people and adults. Born in Worcester, Massachusetts, and educated at Columbia University, he has written or edited for newspapers, magazines, books, radio, television, and films.

Among the many honors for his books are five nominations for the National Book Award as well as the Christopher, Jane Addams, Carter G. Woodson, Jefferson Cup, Washington Book Guild, Olive Branch, and Golden Kite awards. Many of his books have been chosen for the honor lists of the American Library Association, the National Council of Teachers of English, and the National Council for the Social Studies.

The Jefferson life is the latest of eighteen biographies, which include such subjects as Columbus, Washington, Franklin, Mark Twain, Langston Hughes, Mary McLeod Bethune, and Dorothea Lange.

Meltzer and his wife, Hildy, live in New York City. They have two daughters, Jane and Amy, and two grandsons, Benjamin and Zachary. Mr. Meltzer is a member of the Authors Guild.